Shalom: The Search for a Peaceable City

Shalom: The Search for a Peaceable City

Jack L. Stotts

Abingdon Press
Nashville • New York

Library of Congress Cataloging in Publication Data

STOTTS, JACK L. Shalom. Includes bibliographical
references. 1. Peace (Theology). I. Title.
BT736.4.S85   261.8'73   72-6970

ISBN 0-687-38324-2

Scripture quotations are from the Revised Standard Version of
the Bible, copyrighted 1946 and 1952 by the Division of Christian
Education, National Council of Churches, and are used by permission.

Acknowledgment is made of the following material quoted:

Wesleyan University Press has granted permission to quote from
Kenneth Underwood *et al., The Church, The University, and
Social Policy.* The Danforth Study of Campus Ministries. Mid-
dletown, Conn.: Wesleyan University Press, 1969.

Harper & Row, Publishers, have granted permission to use
excerpts from H. Richard Niebuhr, *The Responsible Self.* Harper
& Row, 1963.

Excerpts are used from "Reformation: Continuing Imperative,"
by H. Richard Niebuhr, copyright 1960, *Christian Century
Foundation.* Reprinted by permission from the March 2, 1960
issue of *The Christian Century.*

Quotations from "The Christian Hope and the Modern World"
by Joseph Haroutunian in *Theology Today,* Vol. X, No. 3
(October, 1953) are used by permission of *Theology Today.*

Harper's Magazine has granted permission to use excerpts from
Henry David Aiken, "The New Morals," published in the
February, 1968 issue of *Harper's.*

MANUFACTURED BY THE PARTHENON PRESS AT
NASHVILLE, TENNESSEE, UNITED STATES OF AMERICA

To my wife Virginia

Acknowledgments

A personal word of acknowledgment is in order in introducing the reader to the following pages. Work on this book was made possible by a combined sabbatical and special leave of absence granted by McCormick Theological Seminary. I am grateful to President Marshal L. Scott and the board of directors of the Seminary for this opportunity. Also, a greatly appreciated Faculty Fellowship awarded by the American Association of Theological Schools made this year of study and writing not only possible but also feasible. Mansfield College, Oxford University, extended me its hospitality.

Persons who have stimulated my thought on this subject and contributed to its development are as numerous as the longest "begat" list in the Old Testament. Only a few can be mentioned, however, and I would not burden even them with responsibility for the ideas and expressions contained herein. That remains my own. But my colleagues, particularly John E. Burkhart, Edward F. Campbell, Jr., John F. Dedek, Thomas D. Parker, and Robert C. Worley, will note their influence. Various students have also been cosearchers for adequate ways of thinking about peace. Paul Ridolfi and Phil Zarrilli are two. Two pastors, Frederick R. Trost, who shared leadership with Lewis A. Briner and myself in a seminar on War, Peace, and the Church, and J. Robert Ranck have contributed uniquely to this project and are also representative of many pastors who have shared in reflection on this topic. Dr. Edward M. Huenemann, a friend and cohort, has read the entire manuscript and made very helpful suggestions for its improvement. My wife Virginia typed and retyped and retyped the manuscript, assisted in the preparation of the Index, and maintained, along with our children Stuart, Nancy, and Anna, a state of domestic peace during the time of writing that was, if not that of the eschatological expectation, nevertheless a source of continuing joy and encouragement. To all these and to others unacknowledged by name, *Shalom!*

J. L. S.

Oxford, 1972

Contents

Introduction

A book inevitably has roots in an author's personal history. Perhaps, therefore, a brief word about two elements of my own recent history, both of which have contributed to this study, will assist the reader in beginning to think with me about the search for a peaceable city.

First, in the United States during the last decade the overt concern for peace has swelled to a crescendo. As a professor of Christian ethics in a theological seminary during that time, I could not have ignored, even had I wanted to do so, this mood and activity. As it was, I have been a partisan of the intention and of some of the activity. Further, students and colleagues, churches and "secular" groups, familiar friends and persons known only through the mediation of printed page and television, by their thought and activity, increasingly during the decade provoked and stimulated me to rethink again and again my own understandings and position about what makes for peace. Some did so gently, some abrasively. All contributed. This book is in large part a result of that rethinking. It is not the final word. It is a distillation of a process. It is the report of an attempt to take seriously both the contemporary world and the biblical and theological resources of the Christian faith.

The text that follows is therefore a reflective exercise exploring various dimensions of the Christian faith's self-understanding. While it has risen from, and is directed toward, the practice of faith in the contemporary world, it is also a result of the conviction that, unless such activity is informed and enriched by thought, it is in danger of becoming only reactive to isolated events. In a time of protracted war and rumors of war, of racism and poverty, of ecclesiastical self-doubt and guilt, the search for a peaceable city is too important to be only reactive. Thus the following chapters prompt the church to explore again in depth the full dimensions of its understanding of faithfulness to him whom they confess as the Prince of Peace.

There is a second personal agenda in this study. As a professor of Christian ethics I have been a member of an academic discipline that has itself been no "sea of tranquillity." In recent years there has been extended discussion among my academic colleagues concerning methodological issues. This more obscure and esoteric struggle is the occasion for commenting about a secondary intention embodied in this book. Readers uninterested in this more limited subject can and should skip ahead to the first chapter.

The discipline of Christian ethical thought has recently been dominated in its methodological discourse by what has been called the "rules-deeds" debate. In both Protestant and Roman Catholic circles a renewed consideration has been accorded to the role and standing of "situation" or "context" in moral decision making. Appreciation for the unique nature of individual deeds informed by conscience and immediate situational factors has arisen. But there have also been those who contended for the necessary conformity of certain actions to stated rules and who have argued on behalf of the need for, and the validity of, principles and rules for Christian faithfulness.[1]

It seems to me, however, that this discussion is in danger

12

of becoming sterile by becoming wrongly identified as *the* issue in Christian ethical reflection. If that were to occur, the discussion would subvert its own importance. For there are many issues of importance in the discipline of Christian ethics. Three deserve mention. The first is that of the content of the primary ethical norm to be proposed by the Christian ethicist. The second is a recognition of the socio-cultural experience that shapes both ethical reflection and activity, the Christ-culture question. Finally there is the issue of the broad universe of moral discourse.

In the following pages I have tried to deal with each of these issues, not by entering into debate with other ethicists, but by proposing a constructive argument. For example, instead of *agape* as the primary ethical norm, I have advocated *shalom*.[2] The presupposition is that the latter is preferable both on the basis of biblical and theological criteria and on the ground of adequacy for the contemporary society. Also, I have incorporated into the investigation of theological norm and of operational models an explicit recognition of ways in which the socio-cultural experience affects both the analysis of social reality and the approach to be taken toward reshaping that reality.

A final issue is that of the more encompassing logic of moral discourse that should and can inform the life of faith. This more inclusive consideration is crucial for the ethical task in general and, more narrowly, is required to preserve the rules-deeds discussion from becoming vacuous, disconnected from either legitimate normative concerns or authentic situational components.

The following essay proposes a particular logic of moral discourse for Christian social ethics. Three components are suggested as necessary for inclusion in such a logic. They are (1) a normative proposal, i.e., a theological-ethical symbol that can provide criteria and motivation for individual and corporate activity; (2) an operational model, i.e., a general pattern for social engagement that mediates between the content of the theological-ethical symbol and the contemporary socio-cultural experience and wisdom of the agents, one that welds together human moods and motivations with socio-cultural resources and potentialities to yield humane social policies; and (3) a consideration of strategy available to the agent to effectuate the enactment of social policies that are coherent with the theological-ethical norm. These components interlock, each one affected by and affecting the other two.

With the three components suggested above held in mind, we can briefly preview the methodological *content* of the following chapters. The first three chapters argue on behalf of a particular theological-ethical norm, *shalom*, peace. The appropriateness and validity of this norm are contended for under the rubric of a search for an adequate symbol that can provide meaning and direction for human life.

The extended argumentation on behalf of the need for such a symbol is a function of a widespread uneasiness about the place and validity of religious communities in the contemporary, pragmatic world. Allen Tate is reported to have observed that, "in ages which suffer the decay of manners, religion, morals, codes, our indestructible vitality demands expression in violence and chaos . . . ; men who have lost both the higher myth of religion and the lower myth of historic dramatization have lost the forms of human action. . . . They capitulate from their human role to a series of pragmatic conquests which, taken alone, are true only in some other world than that inhabited by man." [3] If Tate is on the right track, and I believe he is, the dominance of the pragmatic mood and mode is simultaneously a reflection

14

of the loss of humanness and the sign of the need for a re-symbolizing of reality. These first chapters argue for the resymbolization as a crucial role for the faithfulness of the church and for the health of the social order.

But for social ethics, the argumentation for, and the proposal of, a symbol to provide meaning and direction for life are not enough in themselves. That symbol must be geared into the social order by means of an operational model that can effectuate social policies that are in correspondence with the content of the symbol. Such a model, I shall contend in chapter four, is a product of both social experience and social wisdom. It is the former that is emphasized in the text, the assumption being that abstractions such as social policy or social issues or operational models have their roots in the ground of human experience. Social policies advocated and implemented spring full-blown neither from theological-ethical symbols nor from a rational calculation of the dynamics and forms of the social order, though both are crucial. The underlining of the crucible of social experience for shaping social policy positions has seemed a necessary element in the present cultural setting, one where the role of "experience" is being at times uncritically celebrated, at other times ignored.

But the operational model is also the recipient of empowerment by the relationship of the self to the reality pointed to by the theological-ethical symbol. The fifth chapter explores and seeks to illustrate how a theological-ethical symbol has implications for individual and social involvement by affecting both moods and motivations and in legitimating the use of human power.

Finally, chapter six is a strategic proposal for how the church as one human institution can be engaged in relations with "the world."

In each of these interlocked circles of investigation, there are grounds for discussion and disagreement. Some analyses of social power relations might reject, for example, an operational model that seeks transformation through "incremental changes." If that were the case, the proposed logic of moral discourse would not, however, be flawed by such an argument. Indeed, if the evidence were convincing and persuasive, a different model would be adopted. The point is that the logic of moral discourse in social ethics calls for some operational model to be developed. Similarly, the proposed practice of the church's relating to the familial subsystem might be proved in error by more adequate attitudinal influence tests than are now available. But the argument would still be that the church as an institution must find ways of influencing the culture, and that an adequate social ethic must risk informed judgments about particular strategies and practices for the church to follow. Finally, the validity and/or adequacy of *shalom*/peace as a cultural carrier of the good news are open to dispute. But the argument remains that the logic of moral discourse requires some theological-ethical symbol.

As to the fleshing out of the concerns suggested in the text, a great deal of work, of course, remains. What, for example, are the social policies entailed by the search for peace? But an agenda of further thought is a suggestion of work still to be done.

Chapter I
The Search for a
Peaceable City

"There is no such thing as a human heart that does not crave for joy and peace." "After all, peace is the end of this City which is the theme of this work; besides peace is so universally loved that its very name falls sweetly on the ear." "Note, too, that Jerusalem, the mystical name which symbolizes this City, means, as I have already mentioned, 'the vision of peace.' " [1]

St. Augustine, Bishop of Hippo, theologian, restless spirit, writing in the fifth century A.D., characterized man's primary goal in life as a peaceable city. Augustine described such a city as one where men lived in harmony and concord with one another and with God. The boundaries of this city were all-encompassing, and its duration had no end. The peaceable city was the City of God, his gift and man's joy.

Unfortunately, as Augustine goes on to recount, within history the peaceable city is unrealized. Mankind's yearning remains unfulfilled, or, at best, partially realized. The fault lies in man. True, all men seek peace, but some limit its scope. These restrict the residents of the hoped-for city to a limited group, justifying thereby enmity and hostility with the excluded. They define "peace" in terms of limited interests and persons, dividing their fellow creatures into friends and enemies. The result is not harmony and concord but bickering and warfare.

Others seek a peaceable city, but their search is in vain because they do not know what makes for peace. Their energies are misdirected. Believing that peace is attained through the acquisition of such finite goods as material possessions, power, or knowledge, they invest their lives in gaining them. But such acquisitions yield not peace, Augustine observes, but discord and personal emptiness.

As a result of man's misdirected loves, toward either a too limited group or a relative good, there arises within history the city of man, the earthly city, marked by suspicion, fear, a clashing of interests, and injustice. Its boundaries are limited, its citizenry is defined exclusively, and its aims are finite goals which yield no final satisfaction. Thus, within history, Augustine contends, there ensues a constant and continuing tension and conflict between the peaceable city, the city of God, and the earthly city. The church, corporately, and Christians, individually, are marked by the fact that they seek the city of God in the midst of the city of men. Yet even they are not immune from distorting the search for peace and thus disfiguring human life. For all men the two cities are commingled during their earthly pilgrimage.

Because of this intertwining, the maintenance of the tension between the two cities is essential. Otherwise the city of man forgets its authentic destination and settles down comfortably with injustice and enmity.

Augustine ties together the peaceable city with the actual historical situation. In doing so he affirms the necessity for Christians and the church to engage in historical activity that shapes life. For Augustine, no part of God's creation is to be disavowed or labeled as evil and therefore avoided. As R. A. Markus has recently described the Augustinian dichotomy between the two cities, "Loving God or loving something else is oversimplified if taken to mean that the citizens of the heavenly city do not 'love' the objects loved by the citizens of the earthly city. They do. . . . It is the way in which such objects are loved that is in question; whether they are 'used,' and thus valued conditionally, in reference to something else of more ultimate value, or loved to be 'enjoyed,' that is unconditionally, for their own sake." [2] For Augustine all created objects, animate and inanimate, find their ultimate end in God. Only a proper love of God and of all things and persons in God can make for that peace which the earthly city basically desires but of itself is powerless to attain.

What is the nature of the peaceable city? Augustine defines it as the "tranquillity of order." Drawing from Greek, Roman, and Hebrew sources, he projects a classical picture of ordered harmony, one wherein all parts of the commonwealth of creation are in their proper relationship with one another and with their Creator. This peace is known only fragmentarily now. Man's yearning can be only partially realized, both personally and socially. Yet such is the delightfulness and power of the peace that is known that it serves as a stimulant for seeking its expansion, even in the midst of the continuing disorder and deformation of life. With hope in the future as his anchor, and love of all persons and things in God as his way of walking, the Christian moves confidently toward the peaceable city. "And so you see the heavenly city observes and respects this temporal peace here on earth and the coherence of men's wills in honest morality as far as it may with a safe conscience; yea, and so far desires it, making use of it for the attainment of the peace celestial; which is so truly worthy of that name, that the orderly and uniform combination of men in the fruition of God, and of one another in God, is to be accounted the reasonable creature's only peace." [3]

In this last quotation we uncover a source of real mischief within the history of the Christian faith. In the midst of the tension between the peace of the city of God and the peace of the earthly city, Augustine undeniably affirmed that Christians should seek the realization of a peaceable city on earth. Its achievement remained, however, impossible within history. Therefore there creeps into Augustine's thought a subordination of the earthly peace of the city of men to the heavenly peace of the immortality which God has prepared for his people. "But as for our proper peace, we have it double with God: here below by faith, and hereafter by sight. But all the peace we have here, be it public or peculiar to ourselves, is rather the solace to our misery than any assurance of our felicity." [4]

Though it was not Augustine's intention to denigrate Christian activity within history, he nevertheless clearly accorded a secondary place to the peace of the earthly city. Such subordination did not mean exclusion. That later generations of Christians would discount altogether the search for earthly peace as necessitated by their faith was totally inconsistent with Augustine's thought. Yet his way of stating the value of the two forms of peace could clearly be interpreted so as to dissolve the tension between the two and focus attention only on the hereafter.

We can summarize Augustine's positive contention. All men yearn for peace. The peace sought is that of a tranquillity between and among men and God and all of God's creation. It is not a passive state. It is a relationship where the wills of all God's creatures are united in harmony with that of their Creator, where each and all contribute to the well-doing and the well-being of all and each. Despite the buffetings of one self by another, despite the horrific conditions that may prevail as a result of man's misdirected loves, the craving for peace will not be downed. It rises from the depths of the self and the society, an objective condition to be pursued even though such pursuit appears to many as an exercise in folly. Peace with God and man is the external goal of man's basic internal craving. It can only be fully achieved through the gracious love of God known in Jesus Christ. But Christians and the church seek its realization as fully as is possible within history.

Augustine wrote about peace in the midst of a historical period that was itself marked by anything other than the "tranquillity of order." As one commentator has put it, *The City of God* stands between two worlds—that of Graeco-Roman antiquity and that of the Christian Middle Ages." [5] In the collision of disparate interests, world views, desires, and peoples which marks a period of cultural crisis, when the familiar Roman Empire was attacked and threatened with extinction, when the shape of an emerging new order of life was unclear, when the old questions and answers could not encompass the new realities, in just such a time, Augustine maintained that peace was the fundamental craving and goal of the self and of society. In spelling out the characteristics of that peace, he provided a charter for the church and its relationship with society that was to endure for centuries.

The conditions that elicited and formed the context for Augustine's reflections are not without parallel in our own time. It is therefore not surprising that another leader of the Christian faith gained a vast audience in echoing Augustine's words. Pope John XXIII, in his encyclical *Pacem in Terris*, "Peace on Earth," ignited the world's imagination with his call to all men of goodwill to join in the struggle for a peaceable city. Without compromising his own conviction that "Peace on earth, which men of every era have most eagerly yearned for, can be firmly established only if the order laid down by God be dutifully observed," [6] he outlined a full range of concerns that were required for peace. These included the provision for, and the protection of, the rights of man, the just ordering of relations within and between nation states, and an international order that would nurture human well-being materially while protecting the world from war. Pope John concluded his very this-worldly understanding of what makes for peace with the wistful warning that "peace will be but an empty sounding word unless it is founded on the order that this present document has outlined in confident hope: an order founded on truth, built according to justice, vivified and integrated by activity, and put into practice in freedom." [7]

Four brief years later the Council convened by John amplified his call for peace, but bordered his warning in black. Meeting in the midst of a world where discord and enmity's signs included a bloody and brutal war in South East Asia, a "global village" where starvation and malnutrition were rampant, a Middle Eastern situation that continued to smolder and occasionally leap into flames that could ignite an East-West military confrontation, Vatican II called upon the nations of the world to arrive at firm and honest agreements that would establish harmony and cooperation in the world. "Otherwise," the Council signaled, "for all its marvelous knowledge, humanity, which is already in the middle of a grave crisis, will perhaps be brought to that mournful hour in which it will experience no peace other than the dreadful peace of death." [8] The peaceable city of men could well be a necropolis, a city of death.

Simultaneously, while other churches also called for the

establishment of conditions that would make for peace, another cry went up. On street after street and in meeting halls throughout the land, a new antiphonal chorus was heard in the United States. "What do you want?" some nameless leader blurted out. "Peace!" came the response. And then: "When do you want it?" The answer ricocheted back, "Now!" After a few such repetitions the antiphonal exchange became a chant, "Peace! Now!" "Peace! Now!" "Peace! Now!"

Neither the clatter of helicopter blades above the jammed streets nor the silent and surly stares of the hostile or un-understanding could smother the cry or diminish the yearning which provoked it. The message was as plain as the cry. Peace is our goal. And the peace sought was not celestial and hereafter. It was a present condition that was desired.

Not only those who joined the peace parades and demonstrations pleaded for peace, of course. Politically, leaders of nations campaigned on peace platforms and were elected. Some of them formulated national and international policies and practices designed to bring about peace. If these too became the objects of discord and dissension, that was more evidence of the deep yearning for peace among persons in the twentieth century.

At other levels, in schools and in homes, young children, adolescents, and adults joined in decorating posters and doodle pads, clothing and jewelry, with a new sign, the peace emblem. Friends and acquaintances exchanged the greeting of "Peace." And in many churches pastors, priests, and people pronounced the blessing of peace upon one another.

In the declining years of the twentieth century, peoples cried out for a peaceable city. In a world unsure of its emerging contours, one marked by tornadic forces of change and a clash of divergent cultures, one weary of war and exposed through electronic devices to the immediacy of killing and the destructiveness of modern weaponry, the cry went forth. It was a human cry, unmarked by parochialism. As such its source was in the human condition, not in any particular religious or theological perspective. And it was not only a cry. It was an assertion of a commitment to a different form of life than was being currently experienced. Peace represented not only a prerequisite for beginning to live, but a quality of life to be established.

The twentieth-century cultural climate out of which the cry for peace emerged was not unlike the time of Augustine. Both were times "out of joint." Both were periods of inter-action between diverse cultures. Both were marked by the absence of any "tranquillity of order." Indeed, in the twentieth century at least it may well have been the "bite" of a clearly disordered world that made peace appear so desirable and necessary. For the period was one marked by the horror of political assassinations, the turbulence of urban crises, the presence of a "police riot" at a national political convention, the unavoidable evidence of violence inflicted upon minority groups by deeds undone and by policies consciously perpetrated. Certain names became emblems of the absence of peace as a quality of life—Kent State, Cambodia, Jackson State, My Lai, Watts, and Attica. Deforma-tion of language was evidence of the deformation of commu-nity, as epithets of pig and vermin were exchanged bitterly and arbitrarily. To many, the turbulence wracking the land was so severe that the inevitable result loomed as either tyranny or chaos.[9] The land was filled more with tranquil-izers than tranquillity. Yet in just such a time the cry for peace mounted, mobilizing the hearts of millions and the actions of thousands.

Even the most sanguine should not, of course, forget

Augustine's reminder that the craving for peace is itself subject to distortion. Those seeking the peaceable city in the twentieth century had many motivations. If pressed, they would surely have defined their objectives in diverse, if not opposed, fashion. For many the order sought had nothing to do with advancing mutuality among all persons. They sought the order of the status quo. Others did not know what a peaceable city would look like. Nevertheless the search became a rallying point and a starting point for common discourse and action about its content.

But if the contemporary period shared a similarity with Augustine's era as one of barely controlled chaos, it also differed in one crucial characteristic. For while Augustine and his contemporaries assumed that the question of God and the role of religion were necessary ingredients in the search for a peaceable city, those crying for peace throughout the twentieth-century world shared no such presupposition. In this, the contemporary yearning for peace is in good measure different from both Augustine and Pope John. The major distinction lies in the stated and assumed goals and presuppositions of human action. Both Augustine and John embraced God as man's chief end, affirming that such a goal was a necessary contribution to life in the world. For many committed to the peaceable city today, such talk seems archaic and at times even regressive, certainly not necessary. Whereas Augustine and Pope John could not envision peace on earth without the clarity of what makes for peace derived from the revelation of God and mediated through the Christian church, the peace seekers of the twentieth century, taken as a whole, are not so minded. Whereas both Augustine and John were convinced that the Christian faith provides an antidote to misdirected loves and a motivation for genuine loving activity, many in the struggle for peace were clear that peace itself is a sufficient motivation. In fact for some committed to the struggle for peace the overall effect of the religious influence appeared as opposed to the activity that makes for well-being and well-doing for all persons.

This recognition of differing assumptions about what is required for human acting on behalf of peace represents the emergence of a cultural condition that has been defined as secular in contrast to sacred. It does not deny that in the contemporary struggle for peace those motivated by Christian and other religious commitments have not played an important role. It does note a difference concerning the goal and motivations for acting that mark off a decisive boundary between the assumptions of the fifth century A.D. and the contemporary ecclesiastical leaders and multitudes who are engaging in the search for a peaceable city.

Recently, David L. Edwards, Dean of King's College, Cambridge, wrote that if he were asked to typify the contemporary scene by one word, he would first be tempted to reply, "despair." Upon reflection, however, he suggests that the more appropriate term is "secular." "We can agree now that secularization means the displacement from a society's centre of belief in the eternal God, in the 'after-life' as man's great hope, and in supernatural force as man's great ally. Secularization occurs when supernatural religion . . . becomes private, optional and problematic." [10]

In so characterizing the age, Edwards joined numerous other commentators and theologians. It was Dietrich Bonhoeffer, though, who perhaps better than any other writer put the matter succinctly when he wrote from a German prison, "The movement beginning about the thirteenth century . . . towards the autonomy of man . . . has in our time reached a certain completion. Man has learned to cope with all questions of importance without the God hypothesis." [11] And the contemporary search for peace is a concrete example of the lack of any presumed necessity for a belief in God in order to deal with human life, its issues and problems. Again, that is not to say that religious persons—Christians, Jews, Buddhists, to name but three—do not participate in that search. It is to suggest that such convictions and commitments are not requisite for the movement. God was not its working hypothesis.

A concrete human movement for peace which neither assumes the importance of the question of God, nor presupposes that a religious context is necessary for humane activity, challenges the church even more than do those theologians who describe the age as secular. For such a movement acts out what theologians try to communicate through less persuasive media, that is, that a society does not require a belief in the eternal God, that social movements for an improved order of existence do not require any belief in the "after-life," and that individuals and groups are willing to act without recourse to any supernatural power as their ally. Such movements are direct challenges to the positions espoused by Augustine and Pope John, two highly learned and attractive standpoints. For if the age is genuinely secular, and without remainder, then Augustine and John are both archaic figures, admirable in their thought and person, but of little direct pertinence to a secular age.

More fundamentally, however, the question of secularity is not the issue of whether or not Augustine and Pope John have any contemporary pertinence. The issue is instead that of the nature and function of a church that still confesses Jesus Christ as Lord of Heaven and Earth, calls him Prince of Peace, understands itself as his servant, and prays to God for the reign of peace among men. If the age is thoroughly secular, and should be so, are such previous affirmations simply nostalgic window dressing, the futile whimperings of a people whose time in history has come and gone, but who, like other builders of empires, noble and otherwise, retain their strongest affirmations long after the substance of their position has been eroded? Such groups are quaint at their best, boring and regressive at their worst, and in either case irrelevant to the shaping of history. They have nothing to contribute to the urgent human search for a peaceable city, except the ethical residue left over from an empty faith. Is that the situation and the fate of the church?

This challenge to the religious communities in general and to the Christian church in particular is not one to be brushed off like dandruff from the shoulders of a healthy person, a nuisance but hardly a substantive threat to life. It is a substantive challenge. As such it should not be treated defensively, in the context of the necessity to justify the religious communities' continued existence. The issue posed is rather a genuinely human issue, and by that is meant one that has concrete implications for the well-being and the well-doing of human beings. Can the religious community, that is, for our purposes, the Christian faith, speak and act in a way that is crucial for the construction of a peaceable city? If not, one of the church's fundamental religio-ethical norms, love of God and neighbor, would require its retirement from the field with grace. We invoke the word *can*, rather than does, to raise a basic issue, that of whether or not a religious community has anything legitimate to say in a so-called secular world, any contribution to make that the search for a peaceable city simply cannot do without. If so, only then may we ask, "Does it do so?" or, "How can it do so?"

To deal with the issue more precisely, we shall examine somewhat more extensively characteristics of a "secular age."

In doing so we turn to a source that is at once incisive, provocative, and influential, Harvey Cox's *The Secular City*.

Cox argues that the term secularization typifies the emerged and emerging cities of the world. It is the name for the context for, and therefore the effective content of, modern life. Cox employs two clarifying terms—pragmatic and profane—to indicate the meaning of secularization. Pragmatic and profane are two particular styles of activity and understanding. Secularization, pragmatic and profane, defines and directs the nature of the contemporary world.[12]

Secularization is an encompassing term. As characteristic of the present epoch, secularization "marks a change in the way men grasp and understand their life together." [13] Negatively it means that the world is freed from religious and quasi-religious interpretations. It denotes the rejection of all supernatural myths and sacred symbols. It is a rejection of the goal of life as the "after-life," and of some supernatural force as man's ally. Positively, secularization means the legitimacy of pluralistic ways of understanding the world, with the consequent relativizing of all religious world views, privatizing them and isolating their pertinence only to limited sectors of the human city. It means man's recognition of this-worldly endeavors as the legitimate focus of his understanding and activity. Secularization represents the displacement of the centrality of the hereafter by the here and now, and the assertion of humanism, understood as man's bearing responsibility for his actions, and testing those actions concretely by how they affect other men. "The world has become man's task and man's responsibility." [14]

Secularization functions, Cox maintains, as a liberating force. It frees persons to create a humane society and refuses to allow them to assign responsibility to some nonhuman fate or deity. It also denies any attempt by men to absolutize their own society, world view, or value scheme. As a dynamic force, secularization poses problems for social cohesion, but it offers prospects whose outcome can only be discovered in the common search for a common life.[15]

The style of the secular city (by style Cox means the way a society perceives and projects its own self-understanding, "how it organizes the values and meanings by which it lives" [16]) is marked by pragmatism and profanity. Pragmatism refers to how one envisages and solves problems. Profanity refers to the context or frame of reference in which one places issues and concerns.

"By *pragmatism* we mean secular man's concern with the question, 'Will it work?' " [17] The pragmatic style is illustrated and exemplified for Cox by the late President John F. Kennedy, a man who addressed particular and specific issues with great competence and commitment. The pragmatic man, incarnating the pragmatic style, is interested in solving problems, not spinning out comprehensive schemes or utopian dreams. He is restive with any question that does not yield to human intervention and solution. He has no overt concern for unity, for how things hold together or how they cohere. He has an implicit faith, Cox observes approvingly, that the world does hold together, that the solution of a specific problem will be beneficial to mankind. This limited frame of reference is sufficient for the pragmatic man.

Thus pragmatism as a style of life in seeking and living in the secular city directs man's energies and abilities to specific and demonstrable human issues. It rejects the question of unity of vision or activity and ignores questions and issues that involve mystery and awe, that will not bend to human understanding and manipulation. The pragmatic man asks the technological question, "How do we do it?" not that of the reflective thinker, "What does it mean to work?" and/or, "How does this issue cohere with other issues of life?"

Profanity is pragmatism's twin. By profanity Cox underscores the secular-city resident's concern with *this world.* "*Pro-fane* means literally 'outside the temple'—thus 'having to do with this world.' By calling him profane, we do not suggest that secular man is sacrilegious, but that he is unreligious. He views the world not in terms of some other world but in terms of itself. He feels that any meaning to be found in this world originates in this world itself. Profane man is simply *this*-worldly." [18] The profane man does not weep for the disappearance of the realm of mystery; nor does he bemoan the loss of "religion." He rejoices in his neighbor whom he does see, not in any god whom he cannot see. And as for religious practices, nothing goes on really in the temple that is worth talking about. It is not that the sacred and the secular must be held in tension, but that the sacred must retire in order to give free rein to the secular.

In characterizing the secular city as profane and pragmatic, Cox appears to have two agendas. One is that of describing the contemporary world. He recounts and analyzes the nature of the emerging urban, technological society. A second purpose, however, is also present. He is concerned in *The Secular City* that the church corporately and Christians individually should adopt the secular city as their goal, that they should receive their cues for understanding and activity from its dynamics and demands as he has described them. We must consider the adequacy of both description and prescription.

Negatively, one is clear about Cox's intentions. He is opposed to the withdrawal of human energies under religious auspices from the massive human problems that beset mankind. He is anxious to inject the talents and skills of persons

31

into building a more humane society. He is a robust critic of the Christian church's misdirection of its constituents to a world "over-there," and to the church's, or any other group's, attempt to encompass "truth" in a closed system. He is in doing so in the best tradition of the prophetic strain in biblical and American religion, calling the church and individuals to involvement in the world and to compassionate and effective action. Apropos of our earlier discussion, Cox's position rebukes any twentieth-century Christian who would denigrate the search for peace within historical conditions as in any way "secondary" to a so-called religious search for peace outside history.

But the brunt of Cox's argument is more persuasive, perhaps now even to Cox, in what it is opposing in the religious sphere, i.e., an otherworldly, closed-in view of the world, than in what it has proposed as an adequate model for describing and prescribing understanding of, and activity within, the contemporary world. For Cox is not only opposing the Christian and the church's disengagement from building up the humane city of man. In *The Secular City* he is proposing a constructive model of human understanding and activity that calls for accommodation to its shape by Christians and the church. He, along with other proponents of the secular age, is not only laying out the contours for understanding dimensions of the contemporary period. He is proposing pragmatism and profanity as requisite moral obligations consistent with, and required by, the biblical witness to God's intentions. The furthering of these two styles is the way to faithfulness.

But serious questions must be raised about the adequacy of these two styles as sufficient for life within the contemporary world.[19] In doing so we are also questioning whether or not the contemporary period is best characterized by the encompassing term, "secular." Let us first examine pragmatism.

Pragmatic man, as we have seen, directs his full attention to particular and discrete issues. He does not require, is indeed impatient with, a vision of life as a whole. Nor does he need to perceive how involvement in one concern relates to other human problems.

John F. Kennedy was for Cox the exemplary pragmatic man. Numerous articles would support Cox in that contention. President Kennedy apparently gave halting and stumbling answers when queried about his total vision of America. But his energies and talents came alive when he was asked about specific human issues and needs, whether they were in the area of civil rights, economic policies, or international relations. He could bring to bear upon such identifiable issues his impressive intelligence, citing facts and figures, outlining what should be done to "get America moving again."

Like President Kennedy, the pragmatic man works on particular issues and concerns with great enthusiasm and competence. When the question of an encompassing vision is asked, he brushes it aside, anxious to get on with the job at hand. He has an optimistic confidence that what he is doing and can do is worthwhile and will be accepted as such. He is not plagued by questions of mystery or of ultimate meaning. He finds in his current activities sufficient fulfillment for his life and, by faith, the lives of others.

At this point we must hesitate and insert a cautionary note. Does the pragmatist really neither assume nor raise questions about the unity of life or a vision of his and others' destinies? Actually, the pragmatist may assume what he does not wish to question. Indeed, one reason why the pragmatic man feels no need to deal with visions of life as a whole (he calls them visionary), becomes embarrassed with ultimate questions about meaning and purpose, and is impatient with those who question the clear contributions he makes by virtue of his skills and energies, is not that he does not have a sense of wholeness and a vision of how things hold together. He does. He simply assumes it rather than questioning it. The pragmatic man, one who can direct his attention to specific problems and rely upon his own and his colleagues' powers for their solution, is himself one who is firmly ensconced within a world that can be assumed. It is a world that values practical activity, that rewards ingenuity and creativity in solving specific problems, that provides resources for "getting on with the job," and encourages a conviction that each one working individually and in concert with others will contribute to a better world. That faith is the base of the pragmatic man's activity, though he himself would neither articulate its presence nor feel the need to do so.

The pragmatic man, so understood, is not necessarily the pioneer of the new frontier, except in quantitative terms. For he moves self-confidently out of an old settlement. He goes to occupy new territory, to explore new lands, and to carve out new settlements. But he assumes that the new areas will duplicate those from which he came. There may be more of the good things of life than were enjoyed among the already colonized peoples. But the difference is one of degree, not kind. The opening of the new frontier is an extension and expansion of the values of the civilized world. One does not question the legitimacy and adequacy of those values. One moves from strength to strength, to establish more of what he has already known. Of course, quantitatively the pragmatic man questions the attainments of the old civilization. It may not embody enough justice, sufficient freedom, adequate heating, lighting, and food. But he does not radically question the received definitions of justice and freedom and adequate well-being. He is, or may well be, the technologist of the previous city, establishing colonies, not founding new civilizations on new ideals and goals. He extends the boundaries of the old city, so that the new frontiers are constantly being incorporated into the established patterns of life. He is impatient with questions about the unity of life and visions of wholeness because he already has a vision of unity and wholeness implanted in his head and being realized through his endeavors.

To describe the pragmatic man in such a fashion is not to negate or downgrade his activity. It is, however, to suggest he need not be a man of today or tomorrow. Dashing and heroic as he may seem, he could be a resident of yesterday. It is also to suggest that he is not one who has no sense of unity and wholeness as he tackles limited problems. He does. He assumes that coherence which he does not feel it necessary to bring to consciousness, examine, and perhaps alter or transform.

Clearly one strength of Cox's pragmatic man is his commitment to this-worldly activity, to humane solutions to human problems. But one potential weakness is the received frame of reference out of which he moves, a world of values and tasks which he fundamentally accepts. In setting aside the questions of a vision of the whole, in emphasizing action to be done rather than reflection, and in rejecting the realm of mystery, he may reduce life to such a degree that he loses any sense of judgment over his own or his society's activities. The most piercing question to direct to the pragmatic man is not about what he is doing. It is about what he is assuming.

For the unreflective pragmatist may brutalize rather than humanize life. Robert Johann describes this possibility as actual when he writes, "The pragmatism of modern man has, so far, disrupted life more than it has enhanced its values. By viewing life as a set of distinct problems that can be approached piecemeal, instead of as a continuous and comprehensive process all of whose aspects are mutually interdependent, modern man has only succeeded in putting it out of joint. Far from enhancing the world, he has come close to making it uninhabitable." [20] Johann, while affirming the experiential and this-worldly location which pragmatism asserts, argues that the "practical" pragmatists represent too truncated a view of life to deal adequately with human existence. He urges a recognition of the necessity for a consideration of the "quality and coherence of life as a whole." He cites the great pragmatist John Dewey against those who limit pragmatism, as Cox seems to do. "In a complicated and perverse world, action which is not informed with vision, imagination, and reflection . . . is more likely to increase confusion and conflict than to straighten things out." [21]

The issue of the quality and coherence of life as a whole is one of the context within which the pragmatist shall operate. It is a call to balance a "limited pragmatism" with a recognition of the importance of a vision of life, a comprehensive goal, a conviction concerning the quality and coherence of life as a whole. It is such a conviction from which the unreflective pragmatist operates, albeit unconsciously. It is the necessity to examine such a perspective that is not dealt with adequately by defining man as pragmatic within a secular framework.

For some vision or comprehensive perspective is necessary if one is to evaluate particular activities and limited and often disparate goals. Otherwise, on what basis would one decide between, say, John F. Kennedy and George Wallace as exemplary models of the pragmatic style?

The problem with the pragmatic style as an imperative for Christians and the church is not its radicality. It is rather that such a viewpoint may represent a conventional morality, one that is assumed and approved by many within and without the church in America. Such a style may be a function of social and institutional beliefs and practices taken for granted as good. The pragmatic man stands firmly on the foundation of a historical life that embodies coherent value. He is confident of his own activity because he has confidence in the validity and value of his social order. But what happens when events conspire to throw into question not merely the limited task to which one commits himself, but the whole context which has provided a legitimating base for that activity? The question then becomes not, "Does it work?" but, "What does it mean to work?"

Similarly, the profane style of life poses certain problems. The contemporary man is "unreligious," Cox has suggested. And the contemporary world is one where religious rituals and sacred symbols are decorative, not functional. Thus, in a profane time, it is perhaps wise not even to speak of God at all, since such speaking will at this time divert attention from what God intends, the humanizing of life. Further, the profane man relies on his own powers, not on any power beyond himself. He no longer calls on the gods but rallies his powers and accepts his responsibilities and moves toward the secular city. If it is a time for silence about God, it is a time for acting in the world.

Again one identifies with Cox's criticism of religious communities, including Christianity, insofar as they have diverted attention from activity on behalf of observable needs of the neighbor. And Cox is surely correct in analyzing the biblical perspective as one that directs man to take responsibility for the care of the creation. But certain issues remain unresolved. One is similar to the issue raised by the pragmatic style, i.e., the question of ultimate meaning. A second has to do with the relationship of man to any kind of "supernatural force," to use Edwards' term, as man's ally.

The profane man and the profane world reject questions of ultimacy. Robert Johann provides another criticism for our purposes, this one being directed against the too-ready acceptance of a dichotomy between ultimate and penultimate, or sacred and profane. He notes that for many the idea of ultimate refers exclusively to some "super-realm of the really real," which is beyond or above the here and now. It is just such an understanding that Cox adopts in his definition of religion. Clearly the ultimate understood in that fashion is detached from current concerns and interests, devaluing activity in the world. But the term ultimate may also be used to refer to the context of life in which all one's practices and beliefs are set. It is legitimately used as a comprehensive term that does not require escape from the world, but indeed locates this-worldly activity within a comprehensive context.[22]

Dietrich Bonhoeffer similarly warned against the consequences for human life of separating the ultimate from the penultimate, the sacred from the profane. In his *Ethics* Bonhoeffer discusses possible relationships between the ultimate, God, and the penultimate, the profane world of God's creation. He rejects two solutions as illegitimate for the Christian and the church. One he labels "radical." The radical position devalues the penultimate. "Christ is the destroyer and enemy of everything penultimate, and everything penultimate is enmity towards Christ."[23] Those adopting this understanding of the relationship are the objects of Bonhoeffer and Cox's opposition, and rightly so. To the "radicals," what happens in the world is of no importance to God and his followers. They have and seek another city, one which is not of this world.

Bonhoeffer's second position is termed "compromise." The compromise position is the opposite image of the radical answer. For here the penultimate is elevated and the ultimate is excluded. "The ultimate remains totally on the far side of everyday." The ultimate gives free rein to the penultimate, at best justifying what has been done and certifying any human endeavor. In the compromise position, "the world must be dealt with solely by means which are of the world. The ultimate has no voice in determining the form of life in the world." [24]

In both the radical and the compromise style of relationship the ultimate and the penultimate are in a relation of mutual exclusiveness. "Radicalism hates time, and compromise hates eternity." [25] Bonhoeffer says to both perspectives a firm "No." As independent styles or postures toward reality, both are destructive of human life.

Bonhoeffer contends that the ultimate and the penultimate must be held together. He avers, "In Christ the reality of God meets the reality of the world and allows us to share in this real encounter." [26] This encounter does not devalue the profane world. Men require clothing, food, shelter, freedom, and all these are legitimate. But the point is that they may be affirmed as legitimate, more aptly as necessary, human tasks, not in themselves, but precisely because of a conviction and commitment about the true relation between the ultimate and the penultimate known in Jesus Christ. For in Jesus there is no division of reality into a spiritual or sacred as over against a profane sphere. Both are dimensions of the richness of human life. The loss of one diminishes and distorts an understanding of the other.

Bonhoeffer, writing over thirty years ago, in the dark night

39

of man's inhumanity to man, an avid opponent of the Nazi regime, looked out on the social order and its horror, and wrote:

The calling in question of the last things, of the ultimate, which has been taking place to an ever increasing extent during the past two hundred years, has at the same time imperilled the stability of the penultimate, which was closely linked here with the ultimate, and has brought it near to disruption. And in its turn the breaking up of the penultimate has as its consequence an intensified neglect and depreciation of the ultimate. Ultimate and penultimate are closely allied. What must be done, therefore, is to fortify the penultimate with a more emphatic proclamation of the ultimate, and also to protect the ultimate by taking due care of the penultimate. And at the same time there are to be found in western Christendom today large numbers of those who do indeed hold fast to the things before the last, and who are resolved to continue to hold fast to them, but who do not clearly perceive, or at any rate do not resolutely accept, the connexion of the penultimate with the ultimate, even though their attitude to this ultimate is not in any way hostile. In such cases the loss of the ultimate must necessarily lead sooner or later to the collapse of the penultimate as well, unless it is found possible once again to claim this penultimate for the ultimate.[27]

Bonhoeffer's identification of large numbers of those who hold fast to the penultimate sphere without being hostile to the ultimate question parallels Cox's definition of the profane style as one that is "unreligious." The difference is that for Bonhoeffer the consequences of such a stance are finally negative for man himself. For the penultimate loses its moorings without a context that will evaluate and support it. As that occurs the penultimate, the profane world, crashes down around its builders. Thus, to recommend the profane style of life as requisite for Christians and the church may be useful and even necessary as a balance to any emphasis on the ultimate as a realm of reality separate from the here and now. But unless there is a provision for the ultimate as a legitimate consideration of the comprehensive context for life, the profane is, like the pragmatic, robbed of a frame of reference that accords it meaning and purpose. It is not sufficient to be simply this-worldy if one is concerned for the welfare of man. For there are many definitions of what constitutes "this-world." It has been and is a task of the religious community to profer such interpretations.

We can advance our discussion of the necessity of an ultimate context for life and initiate a consideration of the contemporary man's need for any relationship to a "super-natural force" by considering the term transcendent. Now the transcendent in Christian theology does not mean that which is isolated from man, but that which stands over against man. The transcendent refers to the church's conviction that God is not to be identified with man, but it does not mean that God is separated from man. For God to be transcendent means that the God who is worshiped and served is in a relationship with man which is not subject to human control. The transcendent in Christian faith refers to that which is beyond the powers or limits of the human, but not in isolation from the human. The mystery and wonder associated with the transcendent are components of both the "beyondness" and the "presence" of God with his creation. To call God transcendent is to affirm a relationship between the sacred and the profane, the ultimate and the penultimate, not the separation of the one from the other.

Cox himself wishes to hold on to the transcendent as an essential component of modern life. He is anxious that the transcendent not be separated off into that "Super-realm" that is over or beyond or outside of everyday reality. Cox affirms that man experiences the transcendent in a radically this-worldly fashion. In the secular city the self meets the transcendent God in the midst of interaction among men, "where we come up against that which is not pliable and disposable, at those hard edges where we are both stopped and challenged to move ahead." [28]

It appears here that Cox modifies what he had said earlier about profane man. He is not arguing against the transcendent as an important category for human understanding or activity. He is anxious to locate the transcendent in a positive relationship to human activity. But then, is it really accurate to define man as profane without remainder, except as a counterweight to those who deny any positive place for the secular as a legitimate field for meeting and serving the transcendent One?

Similarly, Cox's description of the transcendent encounter as located within human interaction affirms rather than negates the necessary reliance of man upon powers or a power other than his own. Indeed, it appears not inaccurate to say that even for Cox man remains "religious man" if we define the religious man as one who is encountered by a transcendent power and whose comprehensive context of understanding and activity is informed by such an encounter.

Who then is the religious man? He is not, initially at least, one whose being is defined by participation in religious organizations and rituals, though we must not be interpreted as denigrating such. But the religious man is one who knows himself confronted by, and involved with, a sacred power. This sacred power is met and acknowledged within and through human interactions and transactions.

We must be more precise about the phrase, sacred power. First, when we use the word power we mean a reality that has its own force. Second, the modifier sacred indicates that this power is an ultimate power, one that cannot be mastered or manipulated by man. Rather, man is at the disposal of the sacred power.

In the Christian tradition the term God refers to that sacred power who is not so much a "supernatural force that is man's ally" as a fundamental force who reconstitutes human life according to his own intentions. In constituting and reconstituting human life, he graciously invites men to respond to his presence by participating in his purposive activity. This is the God, the sacred power, who is always in relationship with his creation. He may make himself known at the boundaries of life, at times of death, threat of chaos, or fear. But his appearance there is a sign of his appearance everywhere and at all times. Though men may seek to consign God's power and presence only to such boundary occasions, the sacred power affirmed by the church meets man not only in his needs and weaknesses, but also in his struggle for justice, in his affirmation of joy and well-being, and in his search for peace.

For the church, the sacred power meets man within the profane sphere but is not identified with it. Moreover this sacred power is the ground of all human life, the reconstituting force that is always at work. Thus Christians call this sacred power good. God is the name given to that transcendent power who enters human experiencing, providing a ground for affirming that, beyond the disorder of meaninglessness, death, war, and fear, there is a basis for meaning, life, and peace. Indeed, if man has no such experience of a power ordering existence even in the midst of disorder, of judging life in the midst of contentment, of providing for life in the midst of death, of liberating men in the midst of bondage, if he knows nothing of such a transcending power in the midst of the joys and difficulties of life, then he would agree with David Edwards' intitial impulse to name the time as one marked by despair. For despair reflects a human posture toward life that is a function of the absence of any vital conviction about a transcendent power who is both good and powerful.

It is the affirmation of the presence of this sacred power who is reconstituting human life that enables men to live in a disordered world. Men may name the sacred power differently—the urge to humanity, the fundamental evolutionary force, or what have you—but they rely upon some such power as they search for a humane world. For finally, it may be maintained, modern man knows as well as any generation that his own and his neighbors' power is not fully adequate for his own existence. Indeed, in order to maintain his own life with his neighbors he requires not only a fellowman, but a power which sustains and reorders life in the midst of disappointment, death, and betrayal by and of his fellowman. Men still seek a gracious sacred power who can affirm and provoke life in the midst of death, who can enable them to be gracious to an ungracious neighbor, who can reconstitute life even when gracious neighbors are killed or hopes for justice are shattered. This they seek not as an escape from the profane, but as a way of living fruitfully within the profane. For what a sacred power finally provides or may provide is the rooting of life not ultimately within any received social order or social movement or individual characteristic, but in a ground of ultimate power and meaning and direction.

Indeed, without such a rooting for the profane world, men may presume that their particular social order, movement, or characteristics are the ultimate. As that occurs they become not unreligious but idolatrous, locating ultimate power and meaning in limited ends. They build their cities in pride and presume their work to be sufficient in itself. They construct stately monuments and devise master plans. But the city explodes because "what it meant to work" in this-world was defined out of a limited and narrow perspective and with a supposition of the sufficiency of limited powers.

It is questionable, I believe, to identify the contemporary age as only secular, or as primarily secular. It is certainly not inaccurate to identify the pragmatic and the profane as two legitimate and necessary styles of acting in the contemporary world. But to make such patterns of valuing and understanding exclusive of other modes reduces the human experience and enterprise too severely. To propose them as sufficient cues for Christian activity may indeed rob this-worldly, pragmatic activity of what it requires to be truly humane. A consideration of the categories of the pragmatic and the profane suggests that a secular city cannot be or remain genuinely secular, i.e., not idolatrous and dehumanizing, if it is deprived of a transcendent reference by which it may be judged and that may provide some direction for its development and transformation. Further, it needs to hear not only of a transcendent referent. It may well need to hear of a transcendent power who not only affirms human power but also overrules and empowers men to live with humility and hope in the midst of both prideful accomplishments and despairing conditions. This transcendent power must be genuinely transcendent, standing over against what is present, but also in positive relationship with the this-worldly.

Thus, we come to our third consideration, that of the role of a religious community in an age laced with secular moods and styles. Two crucial functions may be noted which a religious community may provide. One is that of maintaining a tension between the limited achievement of man and the purposes of a sacred power for man. It is only such a dialectical tension that may prevent the pragmatic from becoming a fragmenting force in human life and the profane from becoming idolatrous. To recognize this task of holding up and maintaining a transcendent reference does not, of course, argue that the Christian community has done that consistently. That has clearly not been the case. The Christian faith has been understood in a privatized way. It has identified itself with particular cultural achievements, blessing the relative as absolute and justifying the ways of limited groups as the ways of God. But such abuse simply argues the need for a transcendent referent that stands over all religions as well as other cultural systems.

A second function of a religious community and of the Christian faith in particular is to point to and to announce their conviction concerning a sacred power who is the ground and goal of life. There is little of good news in the maintenance of a transcendent reference by which to measure and guide human activity if there is not as well a conviction about an ultimate power who purposefully and persistently fulfills human life individually and corporately.

Two functions that the church can contribute to human life are those of purpose and power. The church contributes to the ongoing life a perspective on the purpose of human life. And it witnesses to a power that is able to bring the purpose to fruition. Its announcement and witness are not the only ones claimant for attention in the contemporary world. But in bringing these concerns to consciousness, the church treats issues that are crucial for human life.

Finally, this witness to a transcendent sacred power will be carried within history by some organization and institution. Its presence in history will surely reflect that it is an earthen vessel. But that recognition, as the apostle Paul urged, itself shows that the transcendent power belongs to God and not to any human institution or movement.[29]

We now return to the human cry for, and movement toward, peace in the contemporary world. While such a movement was obviously not one to assume that the God-question or the issue of the role of religion was crucial for its work, nevertheless the peace movement raised to consciousness what I have identified as religious issues, those of purpose and power. In opposing American involvement in Southeast Asia, for example, articulate members of the peace movement did not do so on the grounds that the national policy simply "wouldn't work," however work was defined by successive national administrations. Rather, the debate occasioned and aroused by the Vietnam War was like that raised by the civil rights movements previously. At its basic level the debate was over the question of the vision and the overarching goal that should inform American policy and practice, about the values and purpose that should shape the national life. It was a call for a transcendent referent that could judge and guide American policy and practice in a more humane fashion than was believed to have been present in the land. It was a call not for an extension of the present value system, but for a transvaluation of values.

I am not contending here that the peace movement in America represented the new church. It did not. What it was doing, however, in calling for a fundamental re-examination of American self-understanding was raising, however inchoately, a religious question, that of a transcendent power that could provide a genuine hope for the reconstitution of the human community. It did so as a human movement, not as a religious movement. But the question raised ought to be recognized for what it was. If such questions are ignored, then the Christian church has nothing to contribute to the search for a peaceable city. But if the search for transcendence, both as referent and power, is a human question requiring some answer toward a humane ordering of the world, then the church has a central role it can and should play.

Indeed Augustine, Pope John XXIII, and the contemporary peace movement may have more in common than we initially thought. While the content of their specific goals may differ, the substance of their concern may coincide. They all seek a peaceable city among men; they all witness to the need for some transcendent reference that can guide in the reordering of the received world; and they all call for peace in the midst of a time "between the times," a time when one period of history is dying and another is struggling to be born. In such a time it is not the religious community which is basically problematic. It is the world itself that is. In such a time the religious question is not posed in narrow sectarian terms. It is a human cry about the purpose of human life and the search for a power proportionate to that purpose.

There is today a search for a peaceable city. But the setting for the search might well be characterized not as a secular city, but as a problematic one. For the actual cities inhabited by man teeter on the brink of breakdown. Isolation between races and classes, a reliance on extremities of armed force, overt and covert violence among peoples, the disparity between the rich and the poor—all these make a humane life a mockery and call for a reordering of human existence. In such a time and setting all persons and groups are called upon to contribute what they have understood to be the purpose of life and the power able to realize that purpose. Christians and the church confess a sacred power who purposes the fruition of all creation and who calls men to participate in the realization of that purpose. To withhold its conviction and commitment from men is to deny the seriousness both of the situation of the human city of man and the positive search for a peaceable city.

Mircea Eliade in *Patterns in Comparative Religion* writes about how all great religions are domesticated. All at their origin affirm a "high God," one who has created the world and is powerful and awe-ful as well as benevolent. But gradually, as life becomes routinized and relatively placid, the high God is removed by men to "another world." Their world becomes secular. The elevation of this high God is, the people say, to preserve his dignity and honor. This high God is gradually replaced by the deities of fertility and creativity, both elements of existence which are necessary for the day-to-day functioning and enjoyment of the ordinary round of life in the world, and both of which are more or less subject to man's control. However, in times of threat and catastrophe, when the orderly life to which a people have grown accustomed is threatened at its roots, then the triviality and lack of power of the familiar gods are blatantly obvious. They can provide no help. Then the high God is remembered and called upon to re-establish his relation with his creation and to preserve the world from chaos. The pragmatic and the profane are inadequate to provide for human life in such a time.[30]

Eliade's account rings a familiar note. Today man's familiar and operative deities (one thinks of sex and technology as convenient parallels to Eliade's categories) are exposed as blatantly powerless to provide for a humane ordering of life. Indeed man recognizes that his creativity (modern weaponry) and fertility (the population explosion) are implicated in the threat of a city of death, not life. At such a time we can at least say that the question of the high God becomes a lively issue. It is that not because of man's weakness but because of his ambiguous strengths. It is that because of a deep desire for a peaceable city that will foster rather than destroy life.

In such a time when human confidence in the "minimal gods" is lost and individuals and groups in either an articulate or inchoate fashion reach out for a high God, religious communities in general and, for our purposes, the Christian community in particular, must find new ways of speaking about and witnessing to the high God whose name they have always borne. They dare not simply repeat the old formulas, whose meanings are overladen with social and cognitive barnacles. But neither can they be silent. They must seek for new ways of speaking and acting, ways that can direct and guide and judge the human reshaping of the world. In doing so they will contribute to the search for a peaceable city.

Thus in a problematic time the Christian faith must find new ways of speaking about, and witnessing to, the sacred power whom it has known in and through Jesus Christ. It must search for and find new symbols that will express its fundamental convictions about the ultimate purpose and power of life, and that will strike a note of authenticity to all those searching desperately for a new order of life. If the call for new symbols appears as an anti-climactic answer to a consideration of what the church can contribute to the search for a peaceable city, we should remember that such a call represents only one responsibility of the church in such a time. But we should also recall that without such symbols the church will exercise no influence and power in the contemporary world.

Chapter II
Symbols and Social Life

Over a decade ago the late H. Richard Niebuhr, in an article assaying his own development and perspective as a theologian, turned his attention to the immediate need of the church and the culture. He wrote:

I look for a resymbolization of the message and the life of faith in the One God. Our old phrases are worn out; they have become clichés by means of which we can neither grasp nor communicate the reality of our existence before God. Retranslation is not enough; more precisely, retranslation of traditional terms —"Word of God," "redemption," "incarnation," "justification," "grace," "eternal life"—is not possible unless one has direct relations in the immediacy of personal life to the actualities to which people in another time referred to with the aid of such symbols. I do not know how this resymbolization in pregnant words and in symbolic deeds (like the new words of the Reformation and the Puritan movement and the Great Awakening, like the symbolic deeds of the Franciscans and the social gospelers) will come about. I do count on the Holy Spirit and believe that the words and the deeds will come about. I also believe, with both the prophets and, of all men, Karl Marx, that the reformation of religion is the fundamental reformation of society.[1]

In a study that followed *The Secular City*, Harvey Cox modified his earlier emphasis on the pragmatic, suggesting that the modern technological society, of which America is the foremost exemplar, suffers from "a surplus of means and a shortage of visions." [2] Furthermore, he registered his conviction that the religious communities can and should provide both ideals and motivation for activity.

Niebuhr's call for resymbolization and Cox's citing of the need for a motivating vision of life reflect a perspective on a fundamental requirement for a problematic world, the necessity of potent symbols. Yet such a perspective found no immediate resonance with the contemporary culture.

Indeed, Mary Douglas, a distinguished social anthropologist, has observed that one of the gravest problems of the present era is its "lack of commitment to common symbols." [3] In fact, she continues, the current scene reflects a deep-seated suspicion of symbols and of rituals associated with symbolic understandings. She echoes Niebuhr's concern as she writes, "the problem of empty symbols is still a problem about the relation of symbols to social life." [4]

Unhappily, it has been the actual concrete relation of certain symbols to social life that has contributed to the current distrust of symbols. For particular symbols have been used to legitimate particular social groups who have maintained exploitive control over others. Just as in earlier centuries the crown and scepter became symbolic rallying points of opposition because of the misuse of the monarchic office, so in recent decades the cross and flag have been identified with the occupation and exploitation of "colonial lands." Or the symbolizing of Jesus as an idealized white Anglo-Saxon racial figure has been associated with the exaltation of one group at the expense of the dignity and well-being of others. The identification of religious symbols with the interests of particular groups reaps a whirlwind of hostility to both group and symbol.

There are other sources of suspicion and indifference about

symbols. One is the high-technology culture that charac-
terizes the present era. This culture has thrived on a matter-
of-fact, no-nonsense approach to life. Its primary language
is empirically oriented. It is a language scheme that leads
to and easily drops over into statistics and mathematical
formulas. Charts and diagrams are its literary deposit. Such
a culture carries a limited view of symbols, associating symbols primarily with written or spoken characters or marks
that have an exact correspondence with that which is immediately verifiable and useful. Thus, the high-technology
culture is highly knowledgeable about quantitative symbols,
i.e., numbers and chemical symbols such as H_2O are its stock-
in-trade. But it is suspicious of, or indifferent to, nonliteral
symbols. Symbols such as God, the kingdom of God, and
justification by faith seem vague, untidy, and "only symbols." Their pertinence for social life seems secondary. The
implication is that such terms could be easily cast aside if
it were not for superstitious and/or sentimental folk.

Also, the rapid change that is characteristic of the high-
technology culture has been and is disruptive of previous
symbols that were embedded in, and meaningful for, particular communities. For in altering patterns of the common
life the high-technology culture dislodged symbols from their
previous communal contexts. Symbols were emptied of their
behavioral and affective content as the communities in
which they had functioned to foster a common life were
subjected to the winds of change. As old symbols seemed
to lose their potency, it was a simple next step to a conviction that all symbols were relatively unimportant. But
the loss of common symbols could be socially deleterious. As
Suzanne Langer has written: "If now the field of our unconscious symbolic orientation is suddenly plowed up by tre-
mendous changes in the external world and in the social

order, we lose our hold, our convictions, and herewith our effectual purposes." [5]

If a high-technology culture gives primary attention to the so-called matter-of-fact or "literal," and relegates concern for the relation of symbols to social life to the dustbin of irrelevance or to the philosophical playroom of secondary concerns, then it does so, however, at its own peril. There is empirical evidence for that assertion. For, as Mircea Eliade has put it, "The most terrible historical crisis of the modern world—the Second World War and all that has followed from it—has effectually demonstrated that the extirpation of myths and symbols is illusory." [6] The symbol of the swastika remains as a bitter reminder that symbols may have degrading and dehumanizing effects. But it is also a reminder that the relation of symbols to social life is an imperative concern for human well-being. What is at stake is nothing less than the quality and perhaps the continuance of social life itself.

There is a convergence here between our earlier argument on behalf of the necessity for the socio-cultural existence of a transcendent referent and the need for resymbolization of religious perspectives. For the religious symbol, which, as Niebuhr has reminded us, carries societal consequences, is a way of stating a conviction about the relationship between the ultimate and the penultimate, the sacred and the profane, the transcendent and the immanent. How one symbolizes the relationship between God and the world is crucial not only for an understanding of God but also for the life of man.

The religious symbol may be defined initially as the verbal intersection where a correlative understanding of God and man converge. [7] Thus, the affirmation of the Protestant Reformation, justification by faith, is a symbolic statement of a certain kind of relationship between God and man. It refers to a kind of interaction between God and man that goes beyond—transcends—human powers and expectations, resting on the activity of a sacred power; but it also points to the way man is to live before God and his fellowman. Or, the kingdom of God proclaimed by the social gospel symbolized the rule of God over and through his creation, and also the goals, attitudes, and ways with which God's creatures were to live in the world.

A task of religious symbols, then, is to provide a referent for correlating the activity of God and man. Its purpose is clearly twofold, to speak of the sacred power and to inform human activity. James Luther Adams, in a provocative essay on "The Pragmatic Theory of Meaning," summarized the focus of the early pragmatists and our concern when he wrote, "The life of man is viewed as essentially a life of action, action in the formation of symbols and action in bringing about practical consequences in terms of the symbols." [8] A religious symbol has practical consequences. Thus, resymbolization and activity consequent on that task are firmly rooted in the human enterprise of creating an acceptable world. They are the attempt to coordinate the purpose and power of men with the purpose and power of God.

Many contemporary theologians have recognized the necessity for rethinking the role and function of symbols. Among them, Paul Tillich has provided a useful catalog of the significance and characteristics of symbols in general, and of religious symbols in particular. A review of his thought can clarify the nature of symbols.

Tillich noted that symbols have a "human nature." That is, any talk about God must employ human, i.e., finite and limited, terms to refer to what is transcendent and infinite. The symbol GOD is a human word that stands for, points to, represents the sacred power with which men have to do. And for the Christian to say, "God the Father of our Lord Jesus Christ," is a symbolic way of speaking about the relationship that the Christian church affirms as constitutive between God and his creatures. Tillich writes, "There can be no doubt that any concrete assertion about God must be symbolic, for a concrete assertion is one which uses a segment of finite experience in order to say something about him." [9] Thus, any statements about God, his nature, his purposes, his activity, are human statements that point beyond themselves. A statement about God is a genuinely human statement, bearing the marks of ambiguity, vagueness, and potential inaptness, as well as those of signification, concreteness, and aptness. But the symbolic statement is not to be confused with that which is named. It is genuinely symbolic.

The religious symbol is correlative. It is a way of linking the sacred power and mankind. Tillich writes, "Religious symbols are double-edged. They are directed toward the infinite which they symbolize *and* toward the finite through which they symbolize it. They force the infinite down to finitude and the finite up to infinity. They open the divine for the human and the human for the divine." He illustrates his meaning by the use of the symbol Father. If we talk of God as "Father," we use a human term, suggesting a familiar human relationship. In doing so, God is "brought down to the human relationship of father and child. But at the same time this human relationship is consecrated into a pattern of the divine-human relationship." [10] So understood, the religious symbol is a way of speaking simultaneously about man and God.

Tillich argues that one cannot arbitrarily construct a religious symbol. A religious symbol arises within a community that knows itself as having to do with a sacred power that reveals itself in and through the finite and historical activities of that community's life. The symbol arises out of the concrete reality of interaction between God and man. The cross becomes a symbol of God's involvement with man. It could never have been arbitrarily made a symbol.

Thus, the symbolizing and resymbolizing task is one related to a particular slice of historical and social life. To name God as King assumes a referent of kingship within the social and political life of a people. The symbolization of God as King has pertinence only if the word king has some prior and consequent meaning within the social life of a people. Further, the symbol dies when it no longer represents an experiential correlation within a people's life experience. For example, the symbol of God as King has little immediate referent in a contemporary democracy. Its meaning is retained therefore only through historical study and empathy, and then only dimly. Thus the symbol of God as King slowly loses power in the contemporary world. It is not the sacred power that dies. It is the symbol that is drained of potency. This illustration, parenthetically, can assist our understanding of resymbolization. In the quotation at the beginning of this chapter Niebuhr rejected retranslation and called for resymbolization. Why? Because retranslation assumes a continuity of the mode of human experience that was constitutive for another slice of history. "Retranslation of traditional terms . . . is not possible unless one has direct relations in the immediacy of personal life to the actualities which people in another time referred to with the aid of such symbols." Translation or retranslation means that one continues the old symbols but spells out their meaning for a new generation. It assumes a continuity of experience. But a break in the cultural experience requires resymbolization, not retranslation, if there is to be a vital communication of the relationship between the sacred power and people. If the old symbol has little or only marginal affinity or correspondence with the present experience of a people, a people may and should study it and profit from their inquiry. But they should not expect it to evoke and focus purpose and power.

We can put the matter in a somewhat different fashion. Religious symbols are always related to particular communities. The religious symbol is a way of saying something about that community's common experience in terms of its convictions and commitments about its involvement with a transcendent power. But God does not give a community a symbol. He enters into their common experience and affords them a new life, a new sense of purpose and power. The community then symbolizes that life which they have seen and known. The continuity of the community does not rest upon its ability to maintain the symbols it employs. The continuity of the community rests upon its ability to maintain the relationship between the God whom it has known and itself. The way that relationship is symbolized will vary, depending upon the dynamics and vagaries of history. Any unwillingness to engage in the task of resymbolization represents not any faithfulness to God but an overcommitment to one particular slice of historical life. The continuity of a religious community resides not in its symbols, but in its continuing and fresh experience of the presence of God.

I have lingered on the relation of symbols to particular historical communities and circumstances. In doing so I have underscored both the historical and human nature of religious symbols and the circumstances which plead for resymbolization rather than retranslation. The latter point is especially important if the present time is truly problematic and denies the assumption of continuity with previous periods. Of course, we should also note that there is never any absolute discontinuity in historical change. There is always a blending. But one's advocacy of either retranslation or of resymbolization will reflect whether he is persuaded more of the one than the other.

Tillich goes on to define other characteristics of symbols. The symbol is seen to open up levels of "external" reality that otherwise are closed to the self. Art, written or graphic, exposes levels of reality as "real" as scientific investigation. Similarly, the religious symbol discloses dimensions of the world that are open only through such means of communication. Correlatively, the symbol opens up dimensions and elements of the self that correspond to the "external" dimensions and elements of reality. Thus, the cross might be interpreted as opening up elements of the distortion of life by human action—men crucify what is good—and the power of God over such distortion as elements and levels of "external" reality; simultaneously it exposes the self's own implication in evil *and* the possibility of a new life despite that involvement.

Finally, what sets religious symbols apart from others is that their referent is, to use Tillich's term, man's ultimate concern. Other symbols, e.g., the national flag, share certain formal characteristics with religious symbols. Indeed they may become formally religious if their referent, in this case the nation, becomes what is ultimate for the self or group. But the religious symbol authentically transcends all penultimate realms. It is genuinely ultimate. Again we recall that to transcend is not to be separated from, but is to be in a relationship with. The ultimate provides a context for the penultimate.

The naming of the ultimate concern shapes how the namers act. The naming or the symbolizing is not only an exercise in signifying. It is as well an evocation of attitudes and actions toward that which is named. To call another person a pig or a worm is both to express attitudes and to shape and preshape actions. It is also to evoke similar attitudes and actions in the hearers. To call God the enemy is to express and evoke attitudes and actions of a quite different sort and order than to name God as friend. "How we name things and events determines how we will act." [11] The symbol which arises from the interactions of a people has as its target the shaping of the interactions of that same and other people.

Religious symbols, then, are not abstractions that have no relationship to the world of everyday. Rather, they are ways by and through which we organize and focus our individual and corporate experience. To change symbols is to change life.

The theologian is not the only inquirer into the nature and function of religious symbols. Sociologists and anthropologists have accorded them extended analyses. A review of some of their findings will illumine further the significance of religious symbols for the social life of man. These social scientists are not concerned to evaluate the truth or falsehood of any religious statement. Their task is to describe as accurately as possible what functions and roles religions and religious symbols play within a socio-cultural matrix. Though their work is not without its value assumptions, their intention is to clarify rather than prescribe for human society.

The sociologist Robert Bellah has defined religion in the following way: "Religion is a generally orienting symbol system in terms of which the world makes sense." The function of religion is to provide a "more or less stable set of definitions of the world and, correlatively, of the self, so that both the transience and the crises of life can be faced." [12]

Any understanding of religion as a generally orienting symbol system should explicitly recognize that such a system involves the carriers of symbols, i.e., institutions and organizations that preserve, translate, or resymbolize understandings across time and space. Further, Bellah's definition should be unpacked explicitly so that the world's making sense includes both beliefs and behavioral components. That is, "sense" means both beliefs and behavior that are "sensible" in the light of the religious orientation. Finally, the religious function is one that provides an orientation to life that does or should inform, direct, and modify the full range of human behavior.

A religion, so understood, has the function of providing some ultimate frame of reference for the self and his companions and their surrounding environment. Religious symbolization is concerned with imaging the ultimate conditions of existence, whether external or internal. This symbolization creates or contributes to a particular understanding of the world. By "world," I mean that network of interrelationships that man has with himself, with nature, with fellowman, and finally with the mystery of being.[13]

Building upon Bellah's argument I suggest that religious symbols have at least two functions in relation to the social life of man. The social anthropologist Clifford Geertz gives a compact definition of religion as a symbol system, indicating in doing so these two functions. He writes: "A religion is: (1) a system of symbols which act to (2) establish powerful, pervasive, and long-lasting moods and motivations in men by (3) formulating conceptions of a general order of existence and (4) clothing these conceptions with such an aura of factuality that (5) the moods and motivations seem uniquely realistic." [14] The two functions that religion as a symbol system fills for the social life may be isolated as the provision of (1) a general order of existence, and (2) persisting moods and motivations that locate individual and corporate activity within that general order. We shall look at each of these.

The first function of religious symbols in providing a general order of existence corresponds to the definition by Bellah above. Religious symbols therefore are not to be identified with one sphere of life. Their reference is by definition comprehensive of all areas of life. Any attempt to relegate the import of the religious symbol to a limited sphere of life, the church and its practices, for example, results in the symbols and consequent practices becoming nonreligious symbols. This is not to deny that symbols called religious have been identified with a narrow range of practices within, and limited consequences for, the overall social life. But such a squeezing of the symbols results in their social strangulation as *religious* symbols.

This function of ordering comprehensively man's practical engagements with the world suggests that such symbols will lack a definitional precision in terms of their consequences for life. The vagueness of the meaning of "kingdom of God" or "love" or "justification by faith" in terms of direct practical consequences within the various spheres of life in which the comtemporary man lives has often been bemoaned. The lack of immediate relationship between such symbolic terms and what the believer is to do as he moves within the matter-of-fact world of his work, leisure, religion, family, etc., has laid such symbols open to charges of emptiness and irrelevance.

Such charges, while in fact pointing to a problem for the religious believer's life in faith, may have been misdirected.

For the lack of clarity of such symbols may be interpreted at a fundamental level as their very gift to social life. The sociologists Berger and Luckmann have argued persuasively that the self participates simultaneously in multiple levels of reality. "Among the multiple realities there is one that presents itself as the reality par excellence. This is the reality of everyday life." [15] By everyday life is meant the immersion of the self in a world of practical activity that is focused on the here and now. It consists of structures of life, beliefs, and activities that are delivered to the self as objective, out there, enduring. Clearly in the world of everyday the immediate pragmatic mode and mood dominate. "My attention to this world is mainly determined by what I am doing, have done, or plan to do in it. In this way it is *my* world par excellence." [16] This is the realm of commonsense knowledge and activity, though that commonsense fund may be expanded by the results of pragmatic activity. The self accepts this world and its direction and activities, goes about his tasks as that world and he have predefined them, occasionally having his world's geographic or temporal boundaries extended, as when one is promoted from a local to a regional office. But the world of everyday is the here and now, the matter-of-fact round of life that one shares with his recognized and recognizable neighbors. It is a world of shared meanings and behavior.

By the world of everyday Berger and Luckmann mean the world that the self participates in routinely. It is the world of the millions who get up every morning and go about the day's activities in the usual way. It is not a boring world, necessarily. It may be exciting, even thrilling. But it is the common routine. Such a world is often divided into sectors, the family, work, recreation, voluntary associations, etc. But they all are part of the world of every day.

This world of everyday can be interrupted. It indeed becomes problematic when it is no longer able to deal with information or events in terms of the common routine. Such an interruption may be the introduction of a task for which one's skills and experiences have not prepared him. Berger and Luckmann illustrate this with the example of the American automobile mechanic who is confronted with a foreign-made car. His world is interrupted, and he must integrate the new challenge into a previous pattern of operation or enrich his own skills and knowledge in order to deal with what is before him. In either case, the world of everyday soon reasserts itself. The adaptive capacity of the self and his everyday world apparently knows few bounds.

Now the case of the automobile mechanic is a simple one, but it could be paralleled by the nuclear physicist who is presented with a problem that does not lend itself to his previous expectations and knowledge, by the nation that confronts opposition from a previous ally, by a middle-class parent whose children suddenly are discovered to be drug-pushers. The experience is of the same quality. The received reality is challenged and must integrate new information into its paramount reality or else construct a new world.[17] The point is, however, that the world of everyday encompasses the self in activities that are very much pragmatic, informed by technical knowledge that is applied according to the sense that has become common, i.e., the common-sense fashion. In such a seemingly pedestrian and pragmatic world there is a strong temptation to deny consequential reality to those other levels of reality which are separated from general practices. After all, what does the "kingdom of God" have to do with working on a Volkswagen rather than a Ford?

It is at this point that Berger and Luckmann suggest

that there is a decisive place within social life for what they call "significative themes." [18] These themes span spheres of reality and are defined as symbols. At this level the language used "attains the maximum *detachment* from the 'here and now' of everyday life, and language soars into regions that are not only *de facto* but *a priori* unavailable to everyday experience." [19] Yet despite the maximal detachment of such symbols, they by that fact have a crucial role to play. For, the symbols constructed by religion, but not only by religion of course, are not merely highly abstracted from everyday experience, but also impinge upon the world of everyday. It is indeed their detachment that makes them applicable to a wide range of sectors of activity. The "kingdom of God" as a religious symbol may not have any specific direction to give to the mechanic or the parents or the nation. But it provides an orienting context which may have very far-reaching consequences for all spheres of activity. A religious symbol is not a substitute for pragmatic knowledge and activity. It is a context for such knowledge and activity. It is or may be that for all spheres of life. Religious symbolization is therefore not a way of abolishing ambiguity and doubt and uncertainty about what is to be done in the world of everyday, but of providing a context for dealing with them. As Bellah notes, a world made up of completely "discrete, atomistic, and unintegrated moral requirements would be incompatible with an organized personality." [20] The resultant state of affairs would be culturally psychotic. Social life requires a symbol system that can transcend but order disparate, pragmatic activities. Religious symbols provide boundaries and directions that are crucial for both individual and corporate activities.

A religious symbol, then, as a symbol detached from the immediate answers of pragmatic activity, provides a comprehensive orientation for the self and the group. It provides a location for specific questions and issues. A comprehensive orientation means that the fragmentation of activity in various spheres of life need not mean fragmentation of the self. The religious symbol has an integrating function, not in the sense of adapting persons to what is, but of providing integrity, or at least the strain toward integrity, for the self and for the group owning the symbol system. Religious symbols provide a context of meaning, and meaning in this sense is location in a comprehensive framework defined by values and norms of a more general order than specific acts, institutions, and practices.[21]

Religious symbols relate to communities. They bind people to one another. Such a symbol system operates as what Geertz calls an "extrinsic" source of information. By that he means that these symbols are lodged outside the boundary of any particular ogranism. Unlike genes which give directions automatically to individual organic processes, symbols operate in a public world of common understandings and meanings. They are inevitably mediated through institutions and customs. As a community function they therefore "are capable of creating a structure of meanings in which individuals can relate to one another and realize their own ultimate purposes." [22] Religious symbols are decisively corporate in their intentionality. Individuals participate in the shaping of symbols, but religious symbols are social in their consequences.

One further aspect of the social location of religious symbols may be noted here. Anthropological study of so-called primitive tribes and historical investigation of ancient communities generally agree that the religious symbols are woven into the texture of the political, economic, and social life of such peoples. Thus, the religious symbol is inevitably as broad in scope as human activities. In the modern high-technology culture one distinguishing characteristic is the differentiation of social functions and processes, the splintering out of spheres of activity and understanding. Thus, the "religious community" is sectored out as one piece of the social pie, as are the political and the economic realms. In such a culture it is or may be assumed that each sector has its own autonomy. But increasingly we recognize the inadequacy of any such assumption. The naïve assumption that social differentiation meant the isolation of one sphere from all others is being replaced by a recognition that each sphere has fluid boundaries and that what occurs in one "compartment" has ramifications for all the others. Political activity, for example, has direct and indirect implications for the economic sphere. And the industrializing process has ramifications for the natural systems that support life. Similarly, the social location of the religious community as one identifiable component in a social system does not mean that the consequences of religious symbols are bordered by what goes on in religious institutions, for example.

In summary, the formulation of a general order of existence is a function which the religious community can provide for social life. The generality of its provision may be a gift, rather than a defect, *if* it is recognized that the general orientation requires specification within the various spheres of life. That specification is itself at times an arduous task. But it is the placing of proximate acts and practices in ultimate contexts that, frequently at least, makes a religion so powerful socially.[23]

A second function of religion, according to Geertz, is that of providing persisting moods and motivations that shape and inform individual and corporate activity within the general order symbolized. This recognition builds the bridge between the general order symbolized and the persistent activity of agents. The religious symbol system serves an empowering function, focusing, regulating, and channeling the activity of selves. By moods and motivations, Geertz points to different elements of the self. We shall look at these briefly.

Geertz defines motivation as "a persisting tendency, a chronic inclination to perform certain sorts of acts and experience certain sorts of feeling in certain sorts of situation." [24] The self is moved in a tenacious fashion to seek after that general order of existence in which he believes. Geertz suggests that motives are interpreted in terms of the ends toward which they conduce. A person may be said to be motivated by love of the neighbor if he seeks effectively to love the neighbor. And the self's love to others for the Christian is set within a framework of seeking God's purposes. A function of the religious symbol system is to grip the self and the group with a sense of ultimacy that moves them to act in such a way that the ultimate end shapes their immediate behavior. Again, we should emphasize that such motivation toward the maintenance or realization of the general order of existence symbolized is not sufficient to determine what ought to be done in a specific situation. One must draw from a wide range of information in order for motivation to become effective action. Nevertheless, motivation to act in a certain way, toward a certain purpose, is crucial for both individual and corporate life. That central motivation provides identity to the self and to the group as it relates to the surrounding world.

To maintain the centrality of motivation that is related to a religious symbol system is not to deny that men are variously motivated. Nor is it to overlook the fact that human beings do not always act on the basis of what religious understanding and commitment require as determinative for their self-understanding and activity. It is to affirm that a religious symbol system has provided and can provide the central motivation for the self and the religious group. The ethicist and theologian would add, *should* provide. Further, when Geertz connects "certain sorts of feeling" with the performance of certain sorts of acts in defining motivation, he takes into account that motivation is not simply a rational ordering of the will. It involves attitudes as well. To be motivated by the religious symbol of the kingdom of God was, for the social gospelers, for example, not only to intend rationally and willfully the reshaping of life in accord with "democratic practices." It was also to feel compassion for those treated unjustly, to feel strengthened to carry on the struggle for better working conditions for the laboring class in the face of hostility and failure, to experience joy in the accomplishment of goals in correspondence with the order of existence symbolized. Motivation is not just of the will conceived as an independent faculty. It is a bearing of the total self, mind, will, and emotions, toward and within the surrounding world.

A second effect of the religious symbol system for social life is the provision of powerful pervasive, and long-lasting moods. Geertz writes, "Motives have a directional cast, they describe a certain overall course, gravitate toward certain, usually temporary, consummations. But moods vary only as to intensity: they go nowhere." [25] He goes on to suggest that moods are interpreted not in terms of their ends, but in terms of their sources. Thus, a parent is *worried* if his teenage child is very late in returning home from a social event. Or a man is in a state of *despair* if his business has gone bankrupt. Or the nation is gripped by a mood of *anxiety* if its continued existence seems threatened by either external threat or internal disruption. Such moods have finite sources, subject to finite conditions.

Moods may also claim an ultimate source. The Christian affirms that for him one way to understand faith in God is as a powerful, pervasive, and enduring mood of confidence in his power and goodness. This mood rests on its source, what God has done in Jesus Christ to demonstrate his faithfulness and love despite man's enmity and betrayal. It involves, of course, a commitment and conviction on the part of the Christian about the source of life. But it resides in what has gripped him as ultimately real and meaningful in his experience. Thus, when Christians say they trust God, or they have hope, or they have a sense of security in the world, their reference is to continuing moods that rest on what they are convinced God has provided as the ultimate framework for their lives. And if such moods are subject to differing degrees of intensity, as surely they are, they nevertheless are fundamental dispositions of the self which affect his self-understanding and his interaction with his fellowmen, nature, and society.

Similarly a corporate group such as the church may be the bearer of a fundamental confidence in God. Its source, they affirm, is God's own self-disclosure, not as an idea but as a sacred power working effectively to bring life to fruition and inviting his creatures to share in that work. This mood is subject to attack by the penultimate moods of disappointment, grief, despair, sorrow, hostility, and fear, all of which have sources in the surrounding conditions of human life, whether those be of failure, death, loss, or persecution. Such conditions rightly evoke moods that correspond to the external circumstances. But the religious community is one whose fundamental mood has its source in what it believes to be the fundamental conditions of life, the ultimate framework or general order of existence. Its ultimate moods thus are pervasive, powerful, and enduring, able and required to provide a place for other moods. And the alteration or exchange of one set of pervasive and powerful moods by another is a religious "conversion." From despair to hope, for hostility to acceptance—these changes in mood point to a transformation in the fundamental relationship to life.

Popular usage is apt to understand moods as moodiness, as in referring to a person as "very moody" and meaning that he or she is apt to shift from one prevailing emotional state to another without any very clear reason for doing so. As I understand him, Geertz means something entirely different. He is referring quite explicitly to the fundamental stance or disposition of the self or the religious community toward the source of life and also toward all the conditions of life. So understood, mood is more affective than it is rational. Faith as a mood is trust, rather than assent. But it is not irrational.

We should be instructed by one other element of Geertz's understanding of religion. He describes it as a symbol *system*. The term system suggests the following. The religious community uses many symbols to refer to its God and his purposes. The Christian church calls God, among other appellations, Father, King, Lord, Shepherd. It symbolizes his purposes for man in terms of salvation, justification, the kingdom of God, heaven, revolution, freedom. All these symbols and more reflect the richness and the breadth of the relationship that the church affirms and experiences. Such a relationship cannot be encompassed in any one symbol. It therefore is illumined and signified by multiple symbols. The systematic character of the religious symbols is the way that can hold them together.

Of course, in particular times particular symbols become

more powerful than others. Some symbols drop from attention, others become regnant. But the plurality of potent symbols is in our time a function both of pluralistic communities with varying and disparate experiences and also of rapid social change which means that one individual is himself a citizen of various experiences. This recognition of the ascendancy and appropriateness of various symbols at various places and for particular groups does not mean that one symbol rules at the exclusion of others. One may become dominant. The complexity and richness of human life argue against any one symbol being wholly adequate. God the Liberator delivering men from the bondage of slavery and exploitation is also God the Comforter who sustains the people at a time of mourning. And the finite quality of symbols suggests that only a plurality of ways of speaking about the infinite will ever be possible, except for the fanatic who would absolutize his own way.

To describe religion as a symbol system is also to recognize that there are different referents for religious symbols. Some religious symbols may attempt to signify God as he is "in himself." Such words as omnipotent and omniscient could be used. Our interest is in those symbols that indicate God's purposes for his creation, his purposes and intentions. This is a level of symbols that attempts to focus human activity in terms of God's activity. This level of symbolization is concerned with the practice of faith. It is particularly concerned with the ordering of the social life of man. As such, a symbol catching up and directing the corporate aspirations of man is particularly important. Thus we have turned to the social scientists to assist us in understanding how religious symbols have affected and do influence social life.

We can summarize the functions of religious symbols for

social life as suggested by sociologists and anthropologists in the following fashion. Religious symbols provide a general orientation to life. That orientation to life is significant to social life in providing a general directionality for human activity and understanding and a fundamental stance or disposition toward life. This general orientation is persuasive to the total self, affecting the self's understanding of what is real, what is to be sought, and what one's relationship to the source of life is. It has important implications for all of life. "The moods and motivations a religious orientation produces cast a derivative lunar light over the solid features of a people's secular life." [26]

To have said all the above is not to say anything about the truth claims or the legitimacy of any religious symbol. It is to argue that religion as a symbol system has had and does have important consequences for personal and social life. Further, it is to contend that social responsibility does not stand in contrast to symbolic understandings but is dependent upon them. Without some sense of a general order of existence, motivations to achieve that order, and moods to sustain the self in his commitments and activities, human behavior is random and scattered, subject to whims of fancy, enthusiasm, or despondency.

Further, these religious symbols, as we have seen, are carried inevitably by communities. These communities provide a focus for the believers, those committed to the symbols. They have a responsibility to embody in symbols and in actions (rituals, ethical practices, etc.) those relationships to the sacred power that are normative for their being. Such a responsibility requires reformulation of symbols and practices to take into account altered conditions of life. The recognition of the important consequences for social life of religious symbols heightens that responsibility. It underscores that the symbols advanced must have reference to the normative tradition of the faith and relevance to the social order. Further it underscores that the religious situation of man is inevitably connected with the general situation of man. If that is the case, we can illustrate the point by suggesting that the Protestant Reformation was not primarily a reform in the religious sphere of life. It was not a reshuffling of doctrines and liturgies. Rather, the Reformation was a revolution in the way(s) some individuals and groups perceived and responded to their total environment —to themselves, to nature, to fellowmen, and to the mystery of being. Thus, the sixteenth-century Lutheran who knew himself as justified by faith, not works, lived in a different environment from that which he had previously occupied. What was affected was his previous understanding of, and behavior in response to, nature, fellowman, and the mystery of being.

To put this another way, there is necessarily a reciprocal relationship between the religious conviction and the general situation of the human enterprise. Our situation today is, then, both the same and different from all other generations. It is the same in that the religious task involves taking into account the total environment of man's life. Only a kind of historical naïveté or whining self-pity would suggest that we were unique in that regard.

In the resymbolization process, then, the religious community must scan both its normative tradition and the problems and prospects of the contemporary social order. As Tillich and others have argued, one cannot simply invent or impose a symbol upon a people. A symbol has its origin, if not its definition, within historical circumstances. In the sixteenth century, justification by faith had a resonance with a people burdened by a need for forgiveness that could not

be satisfied by emphasizing the judging God and his requirements of good works. And Lewis Mumford has written that
a new language becomes effective only when "it develops
by means of clearer images, the ideas already present in a
more or less latent form in the praxis and spirit of the
people." [27]

For a religious symbol to be potent, it must meet the
following conditions. First, it must be an articulation of a
fundamental understanding of the relationship between the
ultimate—God—and the penultimate—human life and its
environment. The symbol must be true to the experience
this is normative for the religious community. It must refer
the hearer to the sacred power that the community has
confessed and does confess as its transcendent source and
goal. Second, the symbol must be one that resonates within
the culture, focusing, clarifying, criticizing, and formulating
stated and incipient hopes, strivings, and frustrations. This
"fit" between the religious symbol and the cultural hopes
and dilemmas must be one that is not circumscribed by
"religious boundaries." It must be a public, not a private,
utterance. That is, the symbol must be able to address the
concrete yearnings and cries that arise within the wider human community. If the symbol is unable to do so, it remains
parochial and isolating rather than encompassing and humanizing.

Finally, the symbol must be comprehensive in its ability
to inform and illumine a wide range of activities, not just
a narrow sphere of life. It must be able, potentially at least,
to contribute to the reformulation of the entire order of
existence.

Religious communities, we conclude, can and should contribute to social life in and through the elaboration of symbols that are potent in focusing and directing human self-

understanding and activity. This task is pertinent at all times. For, as H. Richard Niebuhr has written,

What is the general idea in such interpretation of ourselves as *symbolic* more than as *rational* animals? It is, I believe, this: that we are far more image-making and image-using creatures than we usually think ourselves to be, and, further, that our processes of perception and conception, of organizing and understanding the signs that come to us in our dialogue with the circumambient world, are guided and formed by images in our minds. . . . With the aid of these symbolic systems we distinguish and relate our pasts, presents and futures; we divide up the world of nature . . . ; we relate these to each other in patterns that are intelligible and somehow manageable. . . . Man as language-user, man as thinker, man as interpreter of nature, man as artist, man as worshiper, seems to be always symbolic man, metaphor-using, image-making, and image-using man.[28]

But it is particularly important to discern and to formulate potent symbols within times of social change, in problematic times, when the order of life is called into question. It is during a problematic time, when the old symbols are drained of energizing influence, having lost their fit with the human experience, that the task of resymbolization must rise to consciousness. Such a task is crucial for ordering life in more adequate and humane ways. David Little has noted, "One of the functions of theology is to try to solve the problem of order by means of the development and elaboration of symbolic categories." [29]

One type of symbol urgently required in a problematic time is that of a transcendent vision of the end and goal of life. Such a requirement is filled by what the Christian community calls an eschatological symbol that refers the self and the social order to its final end and goal. This symbolism provides a people with "general goals and [seeks] to assist men to make the continual transition an increasingly complex system requires." [30] An eschatological symbol is not a master plan. It is "vague," and must be so if it is to invite continual historical activity on its behalf. Its vagueness functions as well to provide judgment upon any human achievements, affirming those that correspond to the end to be fulfilled and negating those that do not. An eschatological symbol is genuinely transcendent, standing beyond while infusing human activity, preventing persons from expecting any absolute fulfillment within history while undergirding activity of a positive sort. It connects the purpose and power of God with the purposes and powers of men.

The Christian community in all its forms profers symbols to its neighbors. It does so no longer as a body holding monopoly rights to symbol creation and proclamation. But the loss of monopoly status does not mean the loss of a responsibility. For the symbol-creating task is carried on not just to meet a social need, as clear as that is. Nor is it just to encourage social responsibility on the part of its constituencies, as necessary as the exercise of social responsibility by the church is. But the symbol-creating task is integral to the church's faithfulness to God. It is an exercise of the love of God and neighbor.

Thus, in faithfulness to God the church inquires about appropriate symbols to express his purpose and power and to fit the contemporary human situation. A survey of the surrounding world reveals many groups and movements seeking a new order. In the United States minorities cry for liberation. In the "third world"—among the poor nations—there is expressed the need for revolution. Many affluent Westerners call for meaning and wholeness. Millions call for bread and minimal shelter and clothing. There is also the call for peace.

The search for a peaceable city represents a human yearning and activity that reverberate around the world. It rises from such disparate conditions as threat and fear, aspiration for a common brotherhood of man, repulsion at the thought or anticipation of wreaking death upon a fellow human being, and hopes for worldwide tranquillity. The word peace has itself already become a symbol of human hopes and aspirations. At times it has been a countersymbol, standing over against symbols such as the national flag and what it represents. But even as a countersymbol it has attempted to point to a new order of existence for men and nations.

The question is, "Can the term peace become an appropriate theological symbol within the Christian symbol system?" [31] Earlier I suggested the conditions for the rise and efficacy of a religious symbol. First, the symbol must be able to articulate a fundamental understanding of the relationship of God to his creation. Second, the symbol must resonate with the current cultural experience, focusing hopes and dilemmas. Finally, the symbol must be able to inform a wide range of socio-cultural activities.

Clearly, the term peace matches the second criterion. That it also matches the third has been indicated by our recognition that the search for a peaceable city seeks more than simply the absence of war. The issue is, then, whether or not the word peace can symbolize for the Christian and the church a fundamental theological ordering of life that is consistent with the normative tradition of the Christian faith. Therefore we must examine "peace" as a theological symbol and turn quite explicitly to the scriptures as a primary source for understanding what God intends for his creation.

Is peace not only a human cry, we inquire, but also a legitimate theological symbol that can be endorsed and used by the Christian community in its contemporary proclamation and teaching? Can it provide a transcendent vision for the reordering of life required in a problematic time? Is it, in theological terms, an eschatological symbol that can communicate the powerful purposes of God for his creation and energize human activity?

Chapter III
Shalom: The Content of the Peaceable City

Wolfhart Pannenberg, a contemporary German theologian, summarizes, as it were, our previous discussion and introduces our current concern. He writes:

Eschatological ideas can be explained as a rationally lucid projection of the conditions for a final realization of human destiny in the unity of individual existence and social interrelatedness. In this sense eschatology is intrinsically rational, although it expresses that destiny in symbolic terms. Symbolism, again, is not necessarily mere fancy. In its own way it may relate to the reality of our ordinary experience. It embraces that reality in its totality of meaning and therefore in another form than, say, scientific language. Thus the symbolic language of eschatology does not refer to a completely different kind of reality from that which we experience, but it articulates the element of mystery in the one world and in the one life which is ours.[1]

The need for eschatological symbols arises from within the human condition. As symbols they express man's search for the fulfillment of his destiny. As religious symbols they express confidence in a sacred power who can bring that destiny to completion. Such symbols direct human activity toward the future. As religious symbols they remain transcendent of human realization, resting finally upon the activity of God for their consummation.

The vividness of, and the urgency for, eschatological symbols become apparent in times of individual and social crises. For the question of the present is inevitably a question of the future. A problematic present makes ordinary such questions as: "Is there a future possible for man?" "Where will it all end?" "What is the vision of the end toward which we are to strive?"

Eschatological symbols arise within the world of everyday, but especially during periods of change and challenge, when the old system of order seems teetering on the edge of chaos and the familiar moods and motivation are threatened by charges of being irrelevant to, or destructive of, human well-being. In such a time the received world of everyday appears as pregnant with new possibilities and/or threatened with corrosive and destructive acids.

There are various responses to such a time. Many feel a sense of helplessness and frustration. Others are exhausted, for, having expended so much of their energies in what they felt were worthwhile enterprises, they have witnessed their investments yield little concrete achievement. Bitterness, not gratitude, has been their payment. Some withdraw. They retire from active involvement with public issues, contenting themselves with minimal gratifications and satisfactions. Still others defensively absolutize the recent past or present. They occupy the utopia of the status quo, and what doubts or anxieties assault their consciousness are subordinated to the celebration of their own "realized eschatology." Some articulate visions of the future, as did Martin Luther King, Jr., for example, in speeches that projected his hope and in actions aimed toward its realization. Perhaps King's "I Have a Dream" speech is as vivid an example of pertinent eschatological symbolizing as we have seen in recent times. Perhaps for most the response is mixed, ranging from bewilderment to anticipation, from confusion to clarity, from a tug toward withdrawal into private enclaves to a pull toward involvement in public issues. But for all, the question of the future impinges upon the present.

In a problematic time the self-conscious question of the present is a self-conscius question of the future. And in such a time eschatological symbols have a crucial role to paly. For the self, individually and with others, lives toward the future. This is illustrated by the psychiatrist Erik Erikson's remark that a sense of identity for the person includes a sense of "anticipated future." An example of this is the adolescent who goes through an "identity crisis" about who he is, resolving that crisis by discovering where he is going in life. The teen-ager's present takes on identity, or a structure of meaning, when the future to which he is committed is not empty, threatening, or otherworldly, but casts a light upon the present, giving it direction, integrity, and discipline. Or as Rollo May has written, "Intentionality is the structure which gives meaning to existence." [2] The self's present activity and self-understanding can only be uncovered by examining what he intends. No matter how inchoate it may be, one's vision of the future affects what he does and who he is in the present. What is true for the individual is also true for a group.

An eschatological symbol, therefore, is a vision of the end toward which we are moving, or are to move. But it is not divorced from the present. A sense of the future impinges on the present, infusing it with anticipations and expectations, informing the moods and motivations of the self and the corporate body as they seek to live in the present. So understood, an eschatological symbol encompasses both quantitative and qualitative dimensions. It embraces all three dimensions of quantitative time—past, present, and future. But it does so in a way that qualifies all three. For example, an eschatological symbol may assure forgiveness for the past, may energize the present, and may provide confidence for the time yet to be. But whatever the gifts, eschatological symbols fulfill their function as they shape current activity and understanding. They hold together rather than separate the present and the future; they link the object sought and the seeking subject.

This connecting of present and future in a dynamic fashion, so that the future vision shapes the present, stands in contradiction to many contemporary assumptions about eschatology which have been rampant in the Christian church. Against some of these assumptions, the secular theologians have rightly railed. These eschatological understandings either relegated the referent of the eschatological symbol to an otherworldly realm, or else individualized the eschatological promise so radically that it concerned only the single self as he made his lonely and arduous way to his eternal reward. On the other hand, those who did emphasize the social character of the eschatological symbols of the Christian faith recently did so in such a fashion as to identify what was historically possible with the eschatological, thereby forfeiting the continuing tension with which an eschatological symbol stands in relation to all human achievements. In the United States the revivalists absolutized the individualistic and otherworldly eschatology, often promoting thereby a narrow, moralistic, and self-righteous believer. The social gospelers too easily identified their real and potential social accomplishments as equivalents to the final Kingdom, and then the hard rocks of disappointment and man's own frustration of his best plans often led to cynicism. Others, broadly identified as promoters of "peace of mind," introduced a form of realized eschatology which enabled the individual to experience the glories of individual tranquillity while ignoring the relationship of God's promises and gifts to the surrounding social order. All of the above shaped activity in the present. The issue is whether or not they did so in a way that is consistent with the fundamental convictions of the Christian community. To answer that question we must turn to the scriptures. For the church they are a fertile source of eschatological symbols that reflect a concern with the fundamental ordering of life.

In turning to the Bible, we find that the concern for eschatological symbols is no stranger to the Old and New Testaments. The people of Israel looked forward to the coming of a Messiah who would establish his rule over all the nations of the world. They had a vision of a promised land flowing with milk and honey. They anticipated the day when righteousness and justice would grace every relationship, when love would be the texture of the common life, when the poor would be lifted up and the proud would be cast down. The prophets recalled the people to such a vision when their eyes and deeds were distracted by other goals. Throughout the Old Testament there was a search for a life that lay ahead and that was a gift of God who would faithfully fulfill his promises.

In the New Testament Jesus Christ, who is for Christians the central reference point in understanding God and his intentions for man, proclaims a kingdom of God where men shall live in love and fellowship one with another, a condition of life where men shall share willingly what they have, whether it be a coat or cloak or companionship on a journey. This is a Kingdom where all the hungry will be fed, the naked clothed, the dispossessed sheltered, and the tears of mourning and pain washed away. It is a Kingdom for which men are willing to die, and in their dying find its power.

There has been much recent discussion about the nature of the eschatological hope that Jesus held and advanced. While I cannot go into all that literature with even a modicum of thoroughness, I shall attempt to outline some of its salient points that are pertinent for our discussion.

The first point to be noted is that there was present in the Jewish culture of Jesus' time a form of eschatological thought that has been called apocalyptic. Apocalypticism had its origins in the Judaistic experience after the people's return from the Babylonian Exile and up to and through the first century A.D. Apocalyptic thought built upon the promises of God elaborated in the Torah and witnessed to by the prophets. Yet it transposed these promises from a genuinely this-worldly orientation to the context of another world, a world separated from historical existence. Apocalyptic thought flourished in a situation where the people of Israel were often victimized by their enemies, where any hope of the rule of God extending from Jerusalem, as the prophets had forecast, seemed a harsh joke, when the balancing out of wrongs suffered and righteousness rewarded within history clearly was an impossibility. Apocalyptic thought thus fed on the absence of meaning within history for a people who had received the promise of God that through them all the nations of the world would be blessed, and that Jerusalem would be the seat of universal wisdom and power. A besieged and weak people were only taunted by such talk. Yet their identity rested in the promise of God and its fulfillment. One way of redeeming the promise was to ignore history as a significant realm for God's activity and look toward a dramatic intervention that would terminate history as experienced and establish a "new world." The apocalypticists were the heirs of a this-worldly eschatological expectation which appeared as a mockery more than an expectation. Their response was to reject history.

In apocalyptic thought there arose a resultant pessimism about the importance of any historical activity on the part of the people. Such a perspective reflected a conviction that God would enter into his creation to destroy once and for all the present evil age and to introduce his direct rule. In such an intervention there would be also a general resurrection of the dead, where all would be judged. For only by such a resurrection and consequent judgment of all, the quick and the dead, could God establish and vindicate his righteousness, prove his faithfulness, and provide for his loyal subjects. Thus, post-history became the realm of significant meaning and fulfillment.

Apocalyptic thought therefore emphasized a sharp dualism between this present evil age and the age to come. It devalued historical activity by God or men as in any way significant, believing that God had withdrawn from active involvement within history. The only hope was in the Day of Judgment. When that day dawned there would come a messianic figure. He is occasionally called the Messiah, more often the "Son of man." The resurrection of the dead would coincide with his appearance. The coming of this Son of man would not mean the enlivening of historical activity or the historical fulfillment of the promises of God to Abraham, Moses, and all subsequent generations. His coming would mean the end of history.

In the book of Daniel, the best-known Old Testament book of apocalyptic thought, Daniel has several visions of the end of time. He is not always able to understand his own visions but must rely on supernatural powers. For example, "When I, Daniel, had seen the vision, I sought to understand it; and behold, there stood before me one having the appearance of a man. And I heard a man's voice between the banks of the U'lai, and it called, 'Gabriel, make this man understand the vision.' So he came near where I stood; and when he came, I was frightened and fell upon my face. But he said to me, 'Understand, O son of man, that the vision is for the time of the end.'" (Dan. 8:15-17.) In the interpretation that follows, the story of the destruction of the rulers of the world is told, a destruction that would come only after the chief ruler of the world had himself wreaked havoc on the earth. No human hand is able to contain this beastly king. Only a dramatic intervention by God will prevail.

One of Daniel's most dramatic visions provides another example. It is of four beasts rising up out of the sea. These beasts exercise dominion over men, ruling by fear, sheer force, and terror. The last beast is the worst of all. Finally, his reign of horror is intersected by God. Daniel's vision inserts the rising up of God as the logical climax to the building up of historical evil. It goes like this:

As I looked,
    thrones were placed
        and one that was ancient of days took his seat;
    his raiment was white as snow,
        and the hair of his head like pure wool;
    his throne was fiery flames,
        its wheels were burning fire.
A stream of fire issued
    and came forth before him;
a thousand thousands served him,
    and ten thousand times ten thousand stood before him;
the court sat in judgment,
    and the books were opened.
I looked then because of the sound of the great words which the horn was speaking. And as I looked, the beast was slain,

and its body destroyed and given over to be burned with fire. As for the rest of the beasts, their dominion was taken away, but their lives were prolonged for a season and a time. I saw in the night visions,

> and behold, with the clouds of heaven
>> there came one like a son of man,
> and he came to the Ancient of Days
>> and was presented before him.
> And to him was given dominion
>> and glory and kingdom,
> that all peoples, nations, and languages
>> should serve him;
> his dominion is an everlasting dominion,
>> which shall not pass away,
> and his kingdom one
>> that shall not be destroyed. (Dan. 7:9-14.)

The lineaments of the apocalyptic vision and interpretation are evident here. The world is ruled and will increasingly be ruled by evil powers. Yet their dominion will be terminated. The agent of that termination will not be the people of Israel as God's chosen ones. It will be a divine figure, "one like a son of man," who will exercise everlasting dominion over all the kingdoms of the earth. Then evil will have been permanently vanquished.

Apocalypticism resulted in a devaluation of historical activity, either of man or God. One of its sources lay in a condition of control by external powers, the sense of powerlessness felt by the people over their historical future and, perhaps, a numbing of historical sensitivities.

This apocaplytic imagery was a form of eschatological symbolism that had credence prior to and during the time of Jesus' life, death, and resurrection. But as a form of eschatological symbolism it had roots in the history of the

people of Israel. A dominant earlier source of such symbolism was the work of the prophets, particularly such forth-
right spokesmen as Amos, Hosea, the Isaiahs, Jeremiah, and
Ezekiel. We must briefly look at their use of eschatology.

Norman Perrin, for one, has argued that certainly from
the time of Amos and Hosea the message of the prophets is
eschatological. He is persuasive in his contentions that the
prophets direct the attention of the people of Israel to God's
saving activity that will blossom in the future. This activity
will be analogous with what God has done in the past and
is doing now in delivering his people from bondage and in
providing them gracefully with what is required for true
life. He remains faithful to his promise that he will establish
his people within history.

For the prophets, God's activity is intimately connected
with historical activity. If one is to understand and respond
to the rule of God, he must look to the rising and falling
of kingdoms in this world, to Cyrus as a servant of God, to
Assyria as a rod of God's anger. He must interpret the intentions of God within the historical dynamics, for history
is the significant realm for both God and man. Exile and
calamity must be understood not as a sign of the rule of
evil, but as God's disciplining of his chosen. The intention
of God remains consonant with his promises to Abraham
and Isaac, Moses and David—that the people of Israel would
be blessed by God in this world and that through them all
the world would be blessed by God.

All these prophets not only interpret God's activity within
the current time, but look forward to his rule in the future.
Perrin writes that the message of the prophets is eschatological. "They proclaim a future and even climactic salvation
activity of God on behalf of his people. . . . Hosea with a new
city into the promised land, Isaiah with a new David and a

89

new Zion, Jeremiah with a new covenant, and Deutero-Isaiah with a new covenant. Their hope is eschatological because this future divine activity is the decisive salvation event." [3]

The eschatological symbolism varies, but its reference is to historical activity and expectations. As one example, Ezekiel's vision of the dry bones refers to a people, Israel, that has been stripped of life, exiled into a strange and foreign land, and for whom there seems to be no future. To a people in such a condition Ezekiel writes:

The hand of the Lord was upon me, and he brought me out by the Spirit of the Lord, and set me down in the midst of the valley; it was full of bones. And he led me round among them; and behold, there were very many upon the valley; and lo, they were very dry. And he said to me, "Son of man, can these bones live?" And I answered, "O Lord God, thou knowest." Again he said to me, "Prophesy to these bones, and say to them, O dry bones, hear the word of the Lord. Thus says the Lord God to these bones: Behold, I will cause breath to enter you, and you shall live. And I will lay sinews upon you, and will cause flesh to come upon you, and cover you with skin, and put breath in you, and you shall live; and you shall know that I am the Lord."

So I prophesied as I was commanded; and as I prophesied, there was a noise, and behold, a rattling; and the bones came together, bone to its bone. And as I looked, there were sinews on them, and flesh had come upon them, and skin had covered them; but there was no breath in them. Then he said to me, "Prophesy to the breath, prophesy, son of man, and say to the breath, Thus says the Lord God: Come from the four winds, O breath, and breathe upon these slain, that they may live." So I prophesied as he commanded me, and the breath came into them, and they lived, and stood upon their feet, an exceedingly great host.

Then he said to me, "Son of man, these bones are the whole house of Israel. Behold, they say, 'Our bones are dried up, and our hope is lost; we are clean cut off.' Therefore prophesy, and say to them, Thus says the Lord God: Behold, I will open your graves, and raise you from your graves, O my people; and I will bring you home into the land of Israel. And you shall know that I am the Lord, when I open your graves, and raise you from your graves, O my people. And I will put my Spirit within you, and you shall live, and I will place you in your own land; then you shall know that I, the Lord, have spoken, and I have done it, says the Lord." (Ezek. 37:1-14.)

The mood and message of Ezekiel's prophecy are quite different from those of the apocalyptic writers. His symbolism refers to a historical activity in which God is engaged. That activity is ground for hope for those who hear. This eschatological symbolism thus serves a direct purpose for the social life of the people of Israel. It provides both for insight into the ultimate ordering of life and also for "moods and motivations" that shape human activity. It does so in a way quite different from that of the apocalypticists—it orients life toward historical activity as significant, toward the activity of God as present within history, and toward God's future activity as decisive for all peoples.

This prophetic proclamation of a rule of God in power in the present and decisively in the future is, according to Perrin, "the true background to the usage of 'Kingdom of God' in Jewish apocalyptic and in the teaching of Jesus." [4] But there are significant differences, as we have noted, for the apocalypticists and for the prophets. An immediate question that arises, then, is that of the usage of eschatological symbols by Jesus.

New Testament scholars generally admit that the term kingdom of God was an eschatological symbol that Jesus employed in his teaching and manifested in his life, death, and resurrection. They as generally disagree on what the kingdom of God meant.[5] Norman Perrin is again persuasive.

After a thorough review of the materials, he poses the following questions: (i) Is the kingdom of God an apocalyptic concept in the teaching of Jesus? (ii) Is the Kingdom present or future, or both, in that teaching? and (iii), What is the relationship between eschatology and ethics in Jesus' teaching?

Perrin replies that the answer is a firm "Yes" to the first question. Jesus utilized apocalyptic imagery and particularly the apocalyptic emphasis upon the final state of the redeemed with God. Thus the familiar passage of Matt. 25: 31-46, where the Son of man comes in his glory and judges all the nations, the quick and the dead, is clearly apocalyptic in its form. Another reference is Mark 13, commonly known as the Little Apocalypse. That passage refers to the end time, when history is terminated and the Lord gathers his own to himself. The end time intervenes when evil has covered the earth, reaching vast proportions.

But Perrin's answer to the second question qualifies his earlier affirmation and sets the apocalpytic imagery into a different context. For Perrin says that the kingdom of God is for Jesus clearly both present and future. It is present in his dealing with his contemporaries, as the power of God is mediated in and through human relationships, i.e., historical activity. This presence of the rule of God in power negates apocalyptic suspicion of, and even hostility toward, historical activity. It bends eschatological imagery away from the present usage—apocalypticism—to its earlier rootage—prophetic understandings. Thus, for example, in Mark and Luke's Gospels the kingdom of God, the final and crucial event of God's saving activity, begins in the preaching of John the Baptist who proclaims one who will come after him more powerful and mightier than he. And it is Jesus who replies to the Baptizer's question about whether he is or is not the one whom Israel expects by healing and exorcism. He tells John's messengers to report what they have seen, that the blind receive sight, the lame walk, lepers are healed, the deaf hear, the dead are raised up, and the poor have good news preached to them (Luke 7:18-23). Those who take no offense in Jesus are blessed. Thus, Jesus points to the present power of God's rule in and through his activity. Clearly this exercise of power is not what John had expected, especially if we take his description of the one who is to follow him as an accurate representation of his thought. According to both Mark and Luke, the one whom John the Baptizer expected was more of an apocalyptic figure, whose "winnowing fork is in his hand, to clear his threshing floor, and to gather the wheat into his granary, but the chaff he will burn with unquenchable fire" (Luke 3:17). But with Jesus the Kingdom is clearly present as powerfully in mercy and love as in judgment.

Thus, Jesus' affirmation of history as a significant location for understanding and responding to God represents a return to the prophetic understanding of the rule of God. This is not only an abstract proclamation of the importance of historical activity. It is an incarnation of God's rule. Perrin writes that in Jesus the kingdom of God, the rule of God, is present in these ways: "the power of demons is broken, sins are forgiven, sinners are gathering into an eschatological fellowship around Jesus. These are truly historical events in that they are present to human experience." [6] Thus there arise around Jesus those who experience and manifest the power of God in a new way. Indeed, it is a world-transforming way, literally transforming their understanding of the ultimate order of life and altering their intentions and directions.

Thus the crucial distinction introduced by Jesus and his

followers into the apocalyptic imagery is a concrete life. It is Jesus himself who is proclaimed as the Messiah, the Son of man, the Son of God, the Lord. His life, teaching, death, and resurrection—his life in concrete relationship with the Father and his fellowmen—are crucial for understanding God's rule for the disciples and the early church. This understanding conflicts with the eschatological expectations of apocalypticism. Thus, while Jewish apocalypticism is a mode of expression that is used by Jesus and the church, it is not determinative for the church's understanding of the relationship between God and man. As Wayne Rollins has written, "Although Jewish apocalypticism may have supplied the church with a mode of conceptualizing or even of perceiving the Christ-event, the primary experience of the event itself constituted the focal point of early Christian consciousness." And again, "In proclaiming Jesus of Nazareth as Messiah, the early church broke ground for the reclamation of history and of 'world' as the locus of God's self-disclosure, thus displacing the fundamental historical pessimism of Jewish apocalypticism." [7] It is Jesus of Nazareth who transforms human expectations. In him God's rule is manifest now and will be manifest through his followers. It has come very near. The writer of the Gospel of John expresses this continuity between the manifestation of God's power in the life of Jesus and in his followers when he describes Jesus as saying, "Truly, truly, I say to you, he who believes in me will also do the works that I do; and greater works than these will he do, because I go to the Father" (John 14:12). The believer's historical life is oriented toward this-worldly activity, even as his Lord's life was.

This reclamation project for historical activity means that Christians and the church look forward to the fulfillment of history, not its termination. They have a role to play in that historical drama. Thus, while Jesus himself may well have expected, as certainly his early followers did, the fullness of the rule of God to come very soon, the fact that he and they were mistaken about the quantity of time to elapse between his resurrection and the termination of history does not mean that his expectation has no pertinence.[8] For the primary expectation to which the eschatological framework points is that of a qualitative sort, the fulfillment of God's intentions and the consequent structuring of human intentions in accord with his purposes. That qualitative eschatological expectation affects the quantitative dimensions, but is not be be equated with either a short time or a long time. The qualitative effect on all dimensions of time—past, present, and future—remains the same. It shapes activity and attitudes within that time.

Thus, I suggest that Jesus instituted an eschatological expectation that saw the rule of God as both present and future. Perrin seems to me correct in urging that Jesus did look forward toward a consummation of that which was present in his own ministry. Jesus' teaching, Perrin writes, "directs attention to what will be involved in the consummation: judgment, the vindication of Jesus himself, the establishment of the values of God, and the enjoyment of the blessings to be associated with a perfect relationship with God."[9] What was to come eschatologically would not be qualitatively different from what was present in Jesus' own dealings with his contemporaries. For it was the rule of God over his creation present in Jesus that would be consummated finally. Faith that God had ruled, was ruling, and would rule obviated the questions of when that rule would be consummated, or where or how. "But of that day or that hour no one knows, not even the angels in heaven, nor the Son, but only the Father" (Mark 13:32). Urgency in response to God is not because there is so little time left. It is because the time is filled with possibilities and potentialities. It is suffused with the powerful presence of God.

Perrin's answer to his third question, that of the relationship between eschatology and ethics, has been foreshadowed. What Jesus' teachings about the form of life to be lived provide for the follower are illustrations of the kind of responses men are to make to God and their neighbors as they live in the tension between the present partial and fragmentary experience of the relationship God gives and intends and the consummation of that relationship. Jesus' parables, sayings, and blessings paint a picture of the life of faith that men are to live. They are representations of life lived under the present rule of God. They are not specific rules. Nor are they ideals. But they point to the form of life Christians are to embody as fully as possible, moving always from a partial to a more complete actualization. But Christians confess that the final consummation is God's gift, even as are the partial and fragmentary realizations they now experience. Yet the person's and the group's activities are not insignificant.

The conclusion of our investigation is that apocalyptic imagery was a link in the chain of eschatological symbolism, but that the eschatological framework advanced by Jesus drew from the earlier prophetic tradition for its content. Jesus' use of the phrase "kingdom of God" was, for example, clearly an employment of an eschatological symbol, but one that provided for dynamic response by persons to God's activity within human interaction. As a symbol of the future it encompassed and shaped the present. It judged what was present, as is clear in Jesus' own attack upon the religious and political leadership of his day. It formed an order of life within which men could currently live. It did not specify what was to be done in the world of everyday. But in representing a new life both "vaguely" and concretely, it elicited responses of faithful obedience in all the sectors of life.

The connecting link between Jesus' eschatological understanding and that of the prophets is important for another reason as well. Not only does it provide a positive orientation toward historical activity. It also helps to provide content for the eschatological framework. For the content of the eschatological is indicated not just by Jesus' teaching and life, but by the tradition in which he stood, that of the "law and the prophets." Thus, when one begins to give flesh to an eschatological symbol such as the kingdom of God, he can and should turn his attention not only to the New Testament, but also to the Old Testament. For there is a relationship of fulfillment, not exclusion, between the eschatological expectations of the Old and the New. Indeed, it is the use of the Old Testament materials which gives added social dimensions to the full range of the eschatological hope of the early church.

Thus, we turn now to a consideration of the eschatological symbol held by Christians. There are many such symbols in the biblical writings, kingdom, house, New Jerusalem being only three that come readily to mind. I have chosen one that particularly fits our time. It is the symbol of peace.

"One could set forth the whole history of revelation—its substance at every stage—in terms of the biblical word which our term 'peace' attempts to render." [10] This quotation is an enthusiastic endorsement of "peace" as a suitable content for the Christian message. But we must explore more fully what "peace" points to for the people of Israel and the early church.

The two words used in the biblical materials and generally

translated into English as peace are the Hebrew *shalom*
and the Greek *eirene*. *Eirene* is the term used to translate
shalom in the Septuagint, the Greek version of the Old
Testament dating from about the second century B.C. It
therefore has its rootage in the meanings designated by
shalom. We find also that the Greek term as it is used in
the New Testament carries over the meaning of *shalom* from
the Old Testament, while adding new dimensions to it. But
the basic and most comprehensive meaning of peace must
be sought first in the Old Testament.

A persistent and pervasive symbol in the Old Testament
materials for indicating the relationship that God establishes
and intends for man, fellowman, and nature is *shalom*. We
ordinarily translate that word as *peace*. It represents in the
biblical texts, however, a broad range of meanings. The
core meaning is that of wholeness, health, and security.
Wholeness, health, and security do not mean individual
tranquillity in the midst of external turbulence. *Shalom* is
not peace of mind, escape from the frustrations and cares
of the surrounding environment. Rather, *shalom* is a particular state of social existence. It is a state of existence where
the claims and needs of all that is are satisfied, where there
is a relationship of communion between God and man and
nature, where there is fulfillment for all creation.

The broad range of meanings characterized by *shalom*
is evidenced by companion terms with which it is regularly
used. Blessing, salvation, righteousness, justice—all these are
paralleled with *shalom*, fleshing out its content. Further, the
application of *shalom* to diverse types of human relations
indicates its broad reference. Thus, *shalom* refers to individual peace, to the health and good life of one person. When
it does so it may mean that that person is blessed with
material well-being or prosperity, protection from the dan-

gers of war, or with many sons.[11] Or, *shalom,* as is normally the case, indicates communal well-being. Often this well-being means surcease from war or victory in battle. But its more positive meaning is a people dwelling together in "harmony, agreement, and psychic community." [12] People living as fellow citizens of a city live in peace where there is among them a common will and a common responsibility of each for all and of all for each. Overall, *shalom* represents an active relationship between and among persons, a positive involvement with others. Eventually, in the prophets, the relationship of peace is seen as one that is to characterize the whole community of creation.

Shalom also refers to the relationship initiated by God. It is God who gives peace. He is its ultimate source. Thus Second Isaiah writes, "I form light and create darkness, I make weal [*shalom*] and create woe, I am the Lord, who do all these things" (Isa. 45:7). Peace describes the relationship that God intends and provides through his presence with the creation.

Another way to indicate the comprehensive character of the term *shalom* is to note its linkage with the word we translate as covenant. Covenant in the Old Testament refers to the relationship entered into between God and his people. God makes a covenant with Abraham (Gen. 12), promising that Abraham will be blessed and that through Abraham all the nations of the world would be blessed. Abraham fulfills his part of the covenant by venturing out into a strange and distant land. Another example is the Mosaic covenant, signaled by the liberation of the people of Israel from bondage and the promise of a land flowing with milk and honey. These gifts of God are matched by the people's acceptance of certain obligations to God, i.e., the Ten Commandments. A covenant involves mutual commitments and obligations.

The term covenant is of a general nature, used for various legal and treaty relationships entered into by the various peoples of the Near East. It marks the formal recognition and adoption of a special relationship between the corresponding members. But a covenant has no specific relational content. That must be supplied by the terms of the covenant.

Shalom is often used in the Old Testament to indicate the relational content of the covenant between God and Israel. Von Rad writes, "The relationship guaranteed by a covenant is commonly designated by the word *shalom* . . . for which our word peace can only be regarded as an inadequate equivalent." [13] This designation of the covenantal relationship as *shalom* gives us the clue that the word "peace" catches up the many facets of the positive life of involvement that men are to have with one another and their Creator. It reminds us that *shalom* refers to the relationships that God originally intended and that he is powerfully seeking in a fallen history. One commentator has suggested that the term covenant of peace (*shalom*) represents the final prophetic insight into the interrelation of God and his people,[14] like the enduring promise of God in Isa. 54:10:

> For the mountains may depart
>   and the hills be removed,
> but my steadfast love shall not depart from you,
>   and my covenant of peace shall not be removed,
> says the Lord, who has compassion on you.

This centrality for the prophets of the term *shalom* as a symbol of the relationships God intends for his people is witnessed to by the struggle that goes on over that term

47706

and its appropriate use. "From Micaiah the son of Imlah to Ezekiel there is a minority of prophets of doom who passionately resist the message of salvation proclaimed by false prophets. In this conflict . . . the catchword upon which everything turns is *shalom*. . . . *Shalom* seems to have been the culminating point of the theology of some prophetic circles, and therefore the term became the center of bitter controversy between two parties." [15] This struggle between the prophets is illustrated by Micah's utter condemnation of those prophets who cry "Peace" when they are fat and well-off, basking in the comforts supplied by their patrons, while ignoring the genuine requirements of *shalom*—justice, compassion, and mercy (Mic. 3:5-9).

Perhaps the most familiar disputation about *shalom* is that detailed in Jeremiah 6. In that chapter Jeremiah warns the people of imminent destruction, even though the official prophets have counseled that the land would enjoy tranquillity. Jeremiah's reasons are plainly put forth. The people have not dealt fairly with one another. They have not kept the obligations of the covenant. They have been greedy for unjust gain. They have not sought a society where righteousness reigned. And the official prophets, the king's counselors, have added insult to injury. Instead of recalling the people to their covenantal commitments, they have comforted and justified the rulers and the ruled. They have called the very absence of *shalom, shalom*. "They have healed the wound of my people lightly, / saying, 'Peace, peace,' / when there is no peace." The dispute clearly centered on the issue of what it is that can properly be described as a relationship of *shalom*, and about what makes for peace.

Over and over throughout the prophetic writings of the Old Testament, it is the prophets' attacks upon the abuses of man by his fellowman, the ignoring of the covenantal

103

obligations, the misuse of power by ruler and priest, the exploitation of the poor and the needy, that paints by negative example what *shalom* is not. Yet there are clear indications of what *shalom* should be. Pederson summarizes this positive content when he writes: "The peace entered upon between human beings consists in mutual confidence; *shalom* is the full manifestation of the city, and if souls are united, then the *shalom* consists in their acting together for their common prosperity." [16]

The goal of life is the city of *shalom*, the peaceable city. Peace does not require intimate or, what has been called in our time, I-Thou relations among all the residents of the city. What it does require is that through all types of relationships there be expressed mutual confidence and responsibility. If these are absent, then, the prophets declare, there is no peace for the city.

The prophets in their debates about the meaning of *shalom* clearly are referring to what will make for peace in their current situation. Their orientation is toward historical activity. They concern themselves with economic and political affairs, as well as with individual dealings. In doing so they emphasize that *shalom* refers to the totality of life, that it means the wholeness of life lived in a relationship of care and concern for all that is. There is no peace with God without peace with and for the neighbor. There is no peace with one neighbor unless there is mutual care and responsibility for all neighbors. The totality of *shalom* among men is an image of the totality of God's power and purpose. And that peace is to be demonstrated in and through the historical life of man.

But the eschatological dimension of *shalom* is not missing from the prophetic consideration. Indeed, some of the most vivid and powerful of the prophetic writings emphasize *shalom* as an eschatological hope. In Micah there is this imaging of peace.

> It shall come to pass in the latter days
>   that the mountain of the house of the Lord
> shall be established as the highest of the mountains,
>   and shall be raised up above the hills;
> and peoples shall flow to it,
>   and many nations shall come, and say:
> "Come, let us go up to the mountain of the Lord,
>   to the house of the God of Jacob;
> that he may teach us his ways
>   and we may walk in his paths."
> For out of Zion shall go forth the law,
>   and the word of the Lord from Jerusalem.
> He shall judge between many peoples,
>   and shall decide for strong nations afar off;
> and they shall beat their swords into plowshares,
>   and their spears into pruning hooks;
> nation shall not lift up sword against nation,
>   neither shall they learn war any more;
> But they shall sit every man under his vine and under
>   his fig tree,
>   and none shall make them afraid;
> for the mouth of the Lord of hosts has spoken.
>
> (Mic. 4:1-4.)

But this and other eschatological expectations stand cheek by jowl in the prophets with a firm attention to historical activity. The eschatological vision has positive consequences for historical activity.

Shalom is clearly in the Old Testament a corporate term in its primary intention and usage. It points to a society characterized by justice, where human well-being is inclusive of all the nations and peoples. *Shalom* includes material prosperity for all, bodily health for everyone, lives of individual happiness and mutuality, and the use of resources for positive human well-being. Where there is *shalom* there is positive involvement of man with his fellowman and with nature. Further, this *shalom*, according to the most resplendent biblical visions, includes amity among the beasts, friendship between man and nature, and the cessation of the travail of the whole universe. It represents the perfect ecology of God, man, fellowman, and nature. It is a comprehensive relational term, symbolizing the proper relationships that ought to exist between and among all that is. It is used by the prophets as a criterion to hold over against current practices, to recall the people to their constituting covenantal obligations and to their destiny. It unites the ultimate and the penultimate, symbolizing the purpose and power of God and the purpose of man to which his powers are to be bent.

In the New Testament we must discuss the term *eirene*, peace, in relation to Jesus of Nazareth. Jesus who transforms the eschatological framework by reference to himself and the rule of God must be seen as the one who brings and promises *shalom* to the world. He is the decisive agent of what was expected and longed for by the prophets. He fulfills their hopes, even as he transforms them. He fulfills Isaiah's expectation of him whose name would be called

> "Wonderful Counselor, Mighty God,
> Everlasting Father, Prince of Peace."
> Of the increase of his government and of peace
> there will be no end. (Isa. 9:6*b*, 7*a*.)

For it was Isaiah who articulated so beautifully the hope that the anointed one, the Messiah, would come and introduce a paradisial peace, that would be an order of the world where all conflicts were resolved and all potentialities realized.[17] How is that hope realized according to the New Testament?

The term *eirene* is laced throughout the New Testament. Like *shalom* it has a wide range of meanings. At a simple level, it is used as a greeting and a benediction. In John's Gospel, the risen Christ comes to his disciples and says, "Peace be with you" (John 20:21). In Mark 5:34, Jesus tells the woman who touched his garment and was healed to "go in peace." But this is not a casual "hello" and/or "good-bye." The term peace as used in these ways indicates a relationship between persons. Jesus' coming to his disciples gives them peace, a sense of wholeness and well-being; and the dismissal of the woman in peace is to signify that she is sent away in a new relationship with her surrounding world, one of health and joy. Similarly when Jesus sends his disciples out into the villages of Israel he instructs them that when they enter a house they must first say, "Peace be to this house!" If the disciples find resident there a "son of peace," then the peace they bring shall remain. But if there is no receptivity, if there is no acceptance of them, no mutuality, then the peace profered shall be withdrawn (Luke 10:1-12). Peace is a relationship to be extended; it can be accepted or rejected. Its presence and promise are signified by the greeting and farewell.

The symbol of peace is related specifically to Jesus. We see this in Luke's Gospel in particular. Luke announces that John the Baptist is to precede one who is, "to give light to those who sit in darkness and in the shadow of death, / to guide our feet into the way of peace" (Luke 1:79). The angels proclaim Jesus' birth with the announcement of the coming of one who brings to earth "peace among men with whom he is pleased" (Luke 2:14). In Luke 19:42, Jesus weeps over Jerusalem because in its rejection of him it had revealed once more that it did not know "the things that make for peace." In all these references and in others, peace, *eirene*, refers to the fullness of the relationship that God intends and makes possible for his creation through Jesus of Nazareth. It indicates the relationship that God intends to exist and that is concretely embodied in Jesus' dealings with his contemporaries.

Eirene also therefore is used to describe positive inter-personal relationships between and among men that are the fruit of the life and work of Jesus. Thus, Paul in his discussion of eating habits among Christians seeks to move the understanding of the Christian life to a deeper level when he writes: "For the kingdom of God does not mean food and drink but righteousness and peace and joy in the Holy Spirit; he who thus serves Christ is acceptable to God and approved by men. Let us then pursue what makes for peace and for mutual upbuilding" (Rom. 14:17-19). And the author of the Letter to the Hebrews urges his readers to "strive for peace with all men" (Heb. 12:14*a*).

Eirene means reconciliation. The peace which Jesus brings breaks down barriers between persons and peoples. It points to the uniting of all men. Thus, the author of the Letter to the Ephesians reminds his readers that Jesus Christ is himself the condition for, and the possibility of, positive inter-action between Jews and Gentiles. "For he is our peace, who has made us both one, and has broken down the dividing wall of hostility, by abolishing in his flesh the law of commandments and ordinances, that he might create in himself one new man in place of the two, so making peace, and might reconcile us both to God in one body through the cross, thereby bringing the hostility to an end. And he came and preached peace to you who were far off and peace to those who were near; for through him we both have access in one Spirit to the Father" (Eph. 2:14-18). The peace of Christ is the reconciliation of men with their neighbors. It is the ending of hostility and the beginning of mutuality. It is the relationship that God intends and provides for his creation (cf. Col. 1:19, 20).

Eirene is also used to refer to the "peace of mind" that God bestows upon persons through Christ. Paul seems to have this in mind in Rom. 15:13, when he writes, "May the God of hope fill you with all joy and peace in believing, so that by the power of the Holy Spirit you may abound in hope." But even this peace of mind of the individual is not to be separated from peace with the brothers and the seeking in hope of the peace of all God's creation.

Finally, the peace which Jesus brings is the authentic gift of God. It is the relationship which God intends to prevail. But the peace that Christ brings is not undisputed. As with the prophetic period, there will be disparate understandings of peace. The disciples are to walk in the peace of Christ. After an extended discourse on love and the keeping of the commandments of Christ, especially the new commandment that the disciples are to love one another as Jesus has loved them, John writes that Jesus said, "Peace I leave with you; my peace I give to you; not as the world gives do I give to you" (John 14:27). The peace of the disciples is the love of the brothers and of Christ. It is to be in Christ. That is the nature of the relationship mediated to them by Christ. That he is their peace means to have accepted his love as the context of their lives and to live in continuing communion with him by living in mutuality, in love, with all men. This peace is a positive involvement of seeking fullness of life for others, even as Jesus Christ did. To do so is to know the peace of God and to share the peace of God. It is a peace which passes understanding, for who can fathom such a life? And who can of his own power lead it? This peace is understandable only as the gift of God.

This *eirene* is a present gift of Jesus Christ to men. It will be extended by his followers. It is to find its consummation in the future. For the peace which men now share through Christ fragmentarily looks forward to the full peaceable city which is to be and which God is effectively seeking. Peace is the content of the covenant fulfilled in Christ and to be consummated by God. "He is our peace," and Christians look forward to the time when "every knee should bow, in heaven and on earth and under the earth, and every tongue confess that Jesus Christ is Lord, to the glory of God the Father" (Phil. 2:10, 11).

From our brief sample of the meanings of the term *eirene* we can see that *eirene* joins with *shalom* as an eschatological symbol that points to a new order of life, which is available now as a foretaste of what will be. We may adopt the term *shalom* as the symbol that points to the continuity between the Old and New Testaments, referring us to the peaceable city that God is seeking. We can now summarize our discussion.

Shalom is the quality of life given and intended by God. The coming of Jesus Christ is for Christians crucial for their knowledge of *shalom*. His birth is marked by the proclamation of "Peace on earth. . . ." He is the Messiah who inaugurates the rule of God which is peace. The character of *shalom* as an eschatological vision is depicted in two well-known biblical passages. First, from the Old Testament, the peaceable city that is to girdle the earth is described in this fashion:

The wolf shall dwell with the lamb,
  and the leopard shall lie down with the kid,
  and the calf and the lion and the fatling together,
  and a little child shall lead them.
The cow and the bear shall feed;
  their young shall lie down together;
  and the lion shall eat straw like the ox.
The sucking child shall play over the hole of the asp,
  and the weaned child shall put his hand on the adder's
    den.
They shall not hurt or destroy in all my holy mountain;
  for the earth shall be full of the knowledge of the Lord
  as the waters cover the sea.

(Isa. 11:6-9.)

In the New Testament the author of Revelation writes:

And I saw the holy city, new Jerusalem, coming down out of heaven from God, prepared as a bride adorned for her husband; and I heard a great voice from the throne saying, "Behold, the dwelling of God is with men. He will dwell with them, and they shall be his people, and God himself will be with them; he will wipe away every tear from their eyes, and death shall be no more, neither shall there be mourning nor crying nor pain any more, for the former things have passed away." (Rev. 21:2-4.)

Jesus Christ incarnates this peace among men. He brings it as a promise of that to which the Ruler of all that is has committed himself. God is actively seeking *shalom* and will powerfully accomplish his purpose. We know this *shalom* only fragmentarily, however. We know it as a promise. We know it as first fruits. We see only bits and pieces of a life of justice and righteousness. There is ample evidence on every side of the distortion and disfigurement of life. But for the Christian and the church the call and gift of *shalom* are the invitation to participate with God in the effecting of peace. Indeed, the Christian can himself never know the *shalom* of God fully until all men know it. For one of the relational meetings of *shalom* is that what affects my brother affects me. But Christians and the church seek the peaceable city, anticipating God's own action as bringing the promise to fulfillment. Christians and the church pre-enact as far as they can the peace that God wills.

Shalom is a comprehensive symbol. Its ramifications flow out over all of life. It has consequences for interior moods and self-understandings and for structures of life. It is not therefore a hollow abstraction, though the implications of the "vague" depictions of *shalom* are not precise. As a religious symbol, *shalom* indicates a general order of existence toward which individuals and groups live. It does not deny the difficulty of man's (both Christians and those not so named) effecting peace in the various sectors of life. It does not deny the stubbornness of evil and the intransigence of man's distorted understandings of what makes for peace. But as a theological symbol it points to the purposes and power of God, to which men are called to respond positively. It links God's purpose and his power with human purposes and powers. As a generally orienting symbol it can provide a direction for, and a limitation upon, human behavior.

As a symbol of God's purpose, *shalom* provides a vision of the future for a problematic time. It orients the self and his companions toward the future, providing a structure of intentionality which affords meaning to life. The issue of purpose is crucial, for, as Gordon Kaufman has put it, "purpose is the inner connection that binds together a succession of temporal moments so that they will eventually realize a previously intended goal." [18] Without purpose the self or the group's actions are as separate beads that roll here and there, held together by no linking chain that can provide form. A problematic time is one in search of a purpose that can provide coherence to life, one in which temporal moments can be linked together toward a new qualitative time as well as being joined in the quantitative order of past, present, and future. *Shalom* as an eschatological symbol offers such a qualitative vision of life.

Shalom as an eschatological symbol stands in contradiction to all life as it is presently realized. It proclaims a universal city where men live in harmony and fellowship and mutual care. In doing so it stands in judgment of what is and promises a new and more inclusive order of the future.

The biblical symbol of *shalom* thus can and should give expression both to a vision of the final realization of human destiny and to immediately practical concerns. It provides a way of envisioning the present in terms of potentialities. It provides a way of connecting the present and the future in a purposive way. It connects a concern for individual existence and for corporate well-being and well-doing. It takes cognizance of man's need for fundamental purposes for his life. It recognizes that such purposes ought to express his fundamental conviction about, and commitment to, an ultimate sacred power. It preserves the judgment between what is and what is promised to be. It affirms that the consummation of *shalom* is only by God's action, but that God has in Jesus Christ graciously called men to participate in his work. *Shalom* points to a transformation of life beyond man's prospects, but it declares the faithfulness of God to his promises as men act here and now.

Again, to affirm that the fundamental directionality of life is toward the peaceable city is not adequate for forming concrete judgments and for specific activity on behalf of such a city. The commitment to *shalom* is specified in the concrete and specific conditions in which man finds himself. The symbol, to be potent, must be translated into the script of every day. As that is done, the writing may be illegible or only dimly reflective of its fundamental purpose. Or it may be luminous of its ground. But one's ultimate commitment and purpose become only concrete in the specific treatment of human issues. What the symbol of *shalom* does, as do other religious symbols, is to sensitize human purposes and the directionality of human life toward truly human dimensions. That is to say, it points men toward the ultimate context of life.

Shalom is an eschatological symbol that arises from the biblical witness to God's purposes and activity. In proposing *shalom* as an appropriate theological symbol for today, I do so with an eye to the following considerations. First, *shalom* is a symbol that is evidently suited to the stated and latent yearnings of the contemporary world. Today men cry for peace with renewed vigor. Second, as an eschatological symbol that rises from within and has attained a breadth of meaning from a historical religious community, *shalom* can out of the experience of a people contribute to defining what makes for peace and what makes for "false peace." For example, *shalom* is a comprehensive symbol in the sense of applying it to God's purposes for all his creation. Thus the peace to be sought, if it is to be authentic, must take into account the needs and requirements of all peoples, as well as recognizing that the care of nature is integral to a genuine peaceable city of man. Or, the peace to be sought must not be limited to individual tranquillity. It must encompass a concern for humane social structures. It must be a peaceable city where the bodies and the spirits of men are nourished. And *shalom* as a positive, affirmative vision of the well-being and well-doing of the creation transcends any definition of peace that would equate it with the "cessation of hostilities." While the end of armed conflict between nations and peoples is ingredient to the *shalom* of God and therefore a condition of life to be vigorously and persistently sought, the peaceable city comprehends a quality of life that refuses to be defined negatively as the absence of armed strife.

Third, *shalom* as an eschatological symbol can provide a transcendent goal for life which is sorely needed by individuals and groups in a problematic time. As a transcendent symbol it can guard against both the presumption and the despair of men, energizing activity and coordinating a rich variety of endeavors that manifest the quest for a peaceable city. Finally, for Christians and the church, *shalom* points to the intentionality of God whom they have known in and through Jesus Christ. Certainly, as I have argued previously, this eschatological symbol has a particular reference to a culture that is disordered and lacking in directionality, to a problematic time, to a people weary of war. But for Christians and the church, the pertinence of the eschatological symbol does not depend upon the "times and the seasons." They know it as a word which is pertinent to every time and to every generation, though the terms they use to describe it and communicate it will vary. The *shalom* that God intends is an open, dynamic category, to be filled in with content again and again by new perceptions of his gifts and will within diverse historical periods.

Shalom therefore registers for Christians their commitment to the search for a peaceable city among men. Their search moves from strength to strength, for they have known the peace of God in Jesus Christ. The dimness of their vision, the frailty of their experience of its presence, the weakness of their extension of this gift—all these are well known and ought to be confessed. Nevertheless, Christians and the church seek to proclaim by word and deed the peace which God has made present and will consummate. That is their faith and their hope. Christians and the church thus join with others in the search for a peaceable city. Vatican II's Pastoral Constitution on the Church in the Modern World may well then have spoken a genuinely ecumenical word when it declared, "The gospel's message of peace stands forth today with new clarity and in harmony with the best efforts and aspirations of mankind." [19] That statement is an echo of the beatitude that goes, "Blessed are the peacemakers, for they shall be called sons of God" (Matt. 5:9).

Chapter IV
Social Policy and the Experience of *Shalom*

"Blessed are the peacemakers."

But peacemaking is not a simple venture. It involves diligent and disciplined action, informed not only by a vision of the future but also by knowledge of the past and present. Through the study and application of the things that make for *shalom* Christian discipleship contributes to the building of the peaceable city.

The late Kenneth Underwood, in a massive study entitled *The Church, the University, and Social Policy*, affirmed the following:

One of the most important things in a person's life is not just seeing a city, an institution, an organization, a social practice, as it is, but being able to see new possibilities in it, being able to participate in shaping a corporate enterprise into becoming something important in the hopes and expectations of others. To talk of social policy is to talk of projecting oneself and others into the future, of being able to achieve goals with others, of being effective organizationally. To teach, to lead worship, to preach in such a way as to enhance the powers of others to participate in the formation of social policy, is seen as one of the most important aspects of being human and being Christian. To claim to be a Christian who loves God and neighbor and not to attempt to be an effective person in the formation of just social policies is to talk nonsense in the modern world.[1]

Underwood reminds us that *shalom* is no abstract idea, separated from the ebb and flow of life. It is, as an eschatological symbol, a liberating and critical perspective on this world. As such it involves those who are gripped by the potency to which it points, the power and purposes of God known in and through Jesus Christ, in the interactions and transactions of their world. As a corporate symbol it reminds us that individual activity always involves social responsibility. The ordering of social life in a more humane direction is the behavioral answer that Christians give to the gift and call of God.

This ordering of life involves what Underwood and others designate as social policy. Social policy is one step removed from adopting specific actions. Social policy is the formulation of, and commitment to, a course of action that will guide and determine present and future activities. It is the commitment by a social body to a stated social goal and to providing the resources for attaining that goal.

A social policy combines goal and resources. One may fault a social policy on the inadequacy and/or inappropriateness either of the formulated goal or of the marshaled resources. An example of a social policy is the so-called "War on Poverty" launched in the United States nearly a decade ago. That social policy advanced an understandable social goal, the elimination of material poverty from the nation, the raising of the income level of millions of citizens to a standard that could provide at least minimal well-being. It was adopted by an identifiable social body, the nation acting through its governmental processes. It also involved the marshaling of resources to realize the stated goal. The Congress legislated a series of bills. New departments were established to administer the policy. Programs were designed and implemented. A social policy came into being. The relative

116

success and/or failure of that policy is not our concern here. The "War on Poverty" was a social policy. It represented a view of reality not just as it was, but as it should and could be. It sought to enlist participation of a broad range of persons in shaping a more humane future.

A social policy does not refer, of course, only to governmental action. All corporate enterprises have social policies. The church as an institution is committed through its various actions to certain social policies for the broader society and for its own institutional life. The old and now somewhat archaic sounding commitment of the church in America to "an integrated church in an integrated society" was such a stated policy a few years ago. Universities adopt policies as to how they are to be governed internally and how they will carry on the educational enterprise. Businesses adopt policies that relate them to their communities in one way or another. And so it goes. Social policy formation and implementation are an ongoing practice for any social body. They are requisite for any group, whether it be newly emerging or long established. At its simplest level, social policy is the effective reply to the questions, "What do you want this city (church, nation, family, neighborhood, business, world) to look like in, say, five years? How do we realize that goal?"

In a dynamic, organizational world such as is characteristic of the twentieth century, social policy formulation is an ongoing task. We not only formulate but also reformulate policies and consequent programs. The feedback loop has become a familiar communications device designed to assure the effective evaluation of the achievement of specific social policies and the adjustment of programs to provide more effectiveness. Or, new information from an information-packed world may call for the junking of previous policies and the development of new ones. In the modern world *shalom* making involves an acute sensitivity to, and involvement with, the ongoing formulation and implementation of social policies, both within and outside the church. Social policy secures the eschatological symbol to the world of everyday.

The lodgment of *shalom* making within social policy tasks removes any vestiges of romanticism that may still cling to our earlier delineation of *shalom*. *Shalom* making is concrete involvement in the arduous responsibilities of constructing a humane social order that pre-enacts *shalom*. As such it inevitably requires risks, conflicts, and defeats, as well as cooperation with others and victories. It includes an active and effective yes-saying to some proposed and actualized social policies and an active no-saying to others. It compels not only attention to one's own particular, limited "station and its duties" but also to corporate policies and enterprises. Thus, parents exercise their responsibility as parents not only in getting their children off to school each morning but also in manifesting concern for the educational policy adopted by the school board. This latter task may require testifying before a budget hearing, or running for a school board position, or participating in a school boycott. Or a physician who is committed to the increase of health among men must exercise his responsibility for that commitment not only in his office as he treats individual patients, but as he seeks social policies that will contribute to the physical health of all. Citizens by their votes and participation in political campaigns affect social policies. The *shalom* makers of the world, so understood, are not always called blessed by their fellow citizens of the city of man. But that was not the promise of the beatitude anyway!

Shalom as an eschatological symbol functions to induce

restlessness and dissatisfaction with the present. Jürgen Moltmann has put it this way: "Those who hope in Christ can no longer put up with reality as it is, but begin to suffer under it, to contradict it. Peace with God means conflict with the world, for the good of the promised future stabs inexorably into the flesh of every unfulfilled present." [2] This "stabbing" is not a deathblow administered to the world, though it does deflate all its pretensions. It is a pricking of the world to realize its potentialities for a peaceable city. It jabs Christians and the church, urging them to participate in the discipleship of social policy. Thus, the obvious differences between social reality as the Christian community currently finds it and the peaceable city that is sought are an energizing force. The future pulls on the present; *shalom* stimulates social policies that will prefigure the purpose of God.

Shalom as a symbol of the purpose and power of God provides a critical perspective, a transcendent frame of reference, on the present and a potent motivation for acting toward the future. "Present and future, experience and hope, stand in contradiction to each other in Christian eschatology, with the result that man is not brought into harmony and agreement with the given situation but is drawn into conflict between hope and experience." [3] Moltmann goes on to suggest that the Christian hope does not seek "to illumine the reality which exists, but the reality which is coming." [4] In this I disagree. The eschatological symbol functions to enlighten what is. Its brilliant assertion of what our prospects are illumines the distortions of the present, as well as stimulating the imagination as to current positive potentialities. Thus, some accepted social policy may be shown to reflect in no way the peaceable city. The Nazi genocidal policy is a vivid example. Or, the commitment to *shalom* may enable persons to envision unthought-of social policies that take the raw materials of the present and mold them into a creative venture.

The contradiction between the eschatological symbol and the current pattern of existence is mirrored in the conflict about social policies that rise out of, and relate to, current existence. The eschatological symbol thus compels moods and motivations for engagement with what stands in contradiction to the fullness of God's intentions. It also assists in discerning the ethical dimension of present movements and practices. *Shalom* informs and stimulates the task of social policy formation and implementation. Such policies as those that provide for arms control between nations, the resolution of specific conflicts between governments, and the provision of just social conditions for the disinherited are ways by which the commitment to *shalom* is ploughed into the ground of historical existence. Social policy concretizes the commitment to *shalom*.

Yet having acknowledged that the task of peacemaking is lodged within the formulation and implementation of social policy, we must now recognize that even agreement on that point does not guarantee consensus among Christians on the nature and content of specific social policies. These differences between and among Christians have many sources. One may be a difference in doctrinal positions. Another may be in the differing data brought to bear appropriately on a human issue. But there is another, perhaps more basic, source. Moltmann has given us a clue to a fundamental difference. He wrote that the eschatological perspective inevitably draws the self into "contradiction between hope and experience." It is the nature of the experience with which the hope of *shalom* collides that affects differing responses to the tasks of social policy.

Those who are gripped by the gift and hope of *shalom*, those who therefore know themselves as called to be peacemakers, do not share a common experience of what that gift and hope mean for themselves and the surrounding environment. A crucial differentiating factor is their cultural experience. Where one stands when he hears and is convicted by the call toward *shalom* affects how he responds to the penultimate reality which impinges upon him and which he now seeks to order in a way different from before. For the religious experience is inevitably a cultural experience. That is, it is influenced by, even as it also influences, the particular experiences, modes of consciousness, societal practices, personal standpoints, and values that are endemic to the self's cultural location.

H. Richard Niebuhr's classic study, *Christ and Culture*, analyzed the variegated interplay between the affirmation of Christ as Lord and the cultural expression of that faith. Niebuhr denominated three motifs that have marked the history of Christian thought and life.[5]

The first answer to the question of the relationship of Christ and culture is one of *opposition*. Those so persuaded —the monastic movement and sixteenth-century sectarians are two examples—are antagonistic toward the received culture. They urge rejection of its practices, abjure cooperation with its policies. Often they withdraw into a separate community, though they can, as in the Peasant Revolution against which Martin Luther wrote, seek the destruction of the alien and hostile culture.

The second motif is one that *identifies* Christ with a particular cultural achievement. Christ as the patron of Western civilization is one example, as is the Christ who is to be identified with any society's best achievements, whether they be cultural arts or the waging of wars.

The third cluster of motifs is united by the attempt to *maintain simultaneously* the differences between Christ and culture and still hold the two together. There is in this position a dialectical relationship between Christ and culture, but one which can cut different channels, Christ-above-culture, Christ-and-culture-in-paradox, and Christ-transforming-culture. The force of all three of these subtypes is to maintain a tension between the call and gifts of God and the present practices and policies of any particular culture.

If we employ these three motifs as illustrative of historical attitudes toward *shalom* making, we find that the first emphasizes separation from, or destruction of, the dominant culture. The second tends to baptize the received culture. The third maintains a tension between Christ and the prevalent culture. But the specific answer individuals and groups have given to the question of the proper relationship between the two has been influenced not only by their particular understandings of the gospel or of the culture, but by their location within that culture. Thus the intensity and depth of the felt "contradiction between hope and experience" have varied for Christians down through the centuries. Some have surely felt the experience of the present time as a complete contradiction to the eschatological hope. But just as certainly there have been those who have collapsed that contradiction into identification. And there have been others, perhaps the largest group, who have found their experience of the present was both in contradiction to, and in conformity with, their eschatological hope. These latter could both affirm and negate elements of their experience, some as consistent with the eschatological hope, others as contradictory.

Rosemary Radford Reuther has provided another typology which is useful in diagnosing the implications for social life of an eschatological framework. She directs our attention explicitly to the cultural experience that shapes responses to the eschatological message. In a study of radical movements arising from both within and outside the Christian tradition, she suggests that there have been three basic patterns of response to God's redemptive work. Each one reflects a different understanding of the world and a different social imperative from the other two. She labels the three (1) "the apocalyptic crisis," (2) "the Great Master Plan," and (3) "the inward journey." [6] The last, the "inward journey," refers to that response to God's work that ignores or negates the external world. The social energy it releases is primarily one of withdrawal from the world—the inward journey seeks the presence of God within the self. Thus, in discussing the relation of *shalom* to the ordering of the world, to social policy, I shall consider only the first two responses.

The first, the apocalyptic crisis, recalls our earlier consideration of apocalyptic thought. Reuther echoes some of that previous discussion. "The apocalyptic view is . . . one born of social extremity and despair." [7] Arising from a cultural experience of deprivation and marginality, it eliminates all nuances of good and evil, denying ambiguity, polarizing good and evil into radical opposites. History is seen to be in the controlling clutches of evil. No compromise with the rulers of this world is possible without being hopelessly compromised. The vindication of goodness can only come about by a dramatic alteration of conditions. This is only possible if there is a decisive intervention in the course of events, unexpected and unsought. The crises engorging the present testify to the need for such a dramatic change and to its nearness. The mood is one of despair and helplessness. "One despairs of progress and change within the present system. The present system [world] is totally corrupt. Salva-

123

tion can only come when the present situation is totally overthrown and a new order founded on opposite principles of life." [8] Reuther insists that, "every movement that preaches the irreformability of the present system and its total corruption, that believes that the only solution is radical overthrow and reconstitution of the world on an entirely new and different basis, is apocalyptic in structure, even if it uses social-scientific rather than religious language." [9]

Reuther's second position is labeled the Great Master Plan. Those who understand the call of God to be cut from this design look to a long-haul struggle. Their thought and action presuppose a process of historical activity that stretches over the horizons, further than one can see. There are no sharp angles on the road, though there are curves and precipices. Polarization and bitter conflict are replaced by a "lover's quarrel" with the rich and wonderful world. Struggle remains, but it is historical struggle, marked by compromise and ambiguity. Persons are motivated to participate in the historical struggle, accepting the world at least initially on its own terms, while combating its evil. God's activity, it is maintained, is present in the processes of history. He is bringing this creation to fruition, not to destruction. He comes in judgment, of course, upon the distortions of life. But the dynamic of his activity is to alter both what is distorted and what has distorted human life. Thus his word is a once historical judgment and historical grace.

The cultural experience of those committed to the Great Master Plan varies considerably from that of those gripped by the apocalyptic crisis. In the former the cultural experience is most often one of "possession, power, and confidence." [10] Those so persuaded of this pathway toward the eschatological Kingdom cannot be characterized as those suffering from oppression or extreme alienation. They are aware of the contradictions between their eschatological hope and their present experience. They are committed to bringing the latter into more adequate alignment with the former. But they are the possessors of position and status within the present system. They are convinced that that cultural system is laced with positive as well as negative components. They are so persuaded not primarily by a rational analysis of external conditions, but by their position within that system. They know that there is a crisis or series of crises within the world. But they are of the opinion that resources are available to resolve such crises and to move toward a more humane order without overthrowing what is, in favor of some unknown or feared that might be. Indeed they hold in their hands the levers of power which they have confidently exercised. They have seen the resultant changes and are convinced that these can be extended. Their experience and hope are marked by both continuity and contradiction.

We must be clear. Those committed to the Great Master Plan do not identify God's intention with their present culture as it is. But their cultural experience of identification with the culture, and its identification with them, affect their critique and response to that cultural system.

Reuther's analysis joins with that of Niebuhr to underscore the recognition that the response of Christians to their culture has been historically pluralistic. Both expose as well the fact that one source of such disparate answers as to what God requires has been differing cultural experiences. It is there that predispositions toward different kinds of peacemaking activities have been formed. A fertile source of disagreement about what was required for the pre-enactment of the eschatological hope lay not only in different cultures, but in the divergent experiences within any one culture. With the pluralisms of cultures down through history, there is little wonder that there has been disagreement and conflict about the strategy required in response to the eschatological expectation. That disagreement and conflict continue today is also no surprise.

Charles West rivets our attention upon the contemporary scene. In a study stimulated by the World Conference on Church and Society held at Geneva, Switzerland, in 1966, West illustrates and documents a fundamental rift within the contemporary Christian community, a cleavage that stretches as well outside its borders. This split is not between those who are committed to the advancement of conditions more nearly approximate to *shalom* and those who identify the present with the peaceable city. It is, rather, between "apostles of development in continuity with the past and the apostles of conscious rejection of forces of the past." At Geneva there was a confrontation that fundamentally, West argues, "was between basically different experiences of where reality lies and what its problems are." [11] West identifies the two groups as the "technologists" and the "revolutionaries." Among the differences between the two groups there is one that stands out for our purposes. "The technologist," West writes, "starts from the experience of an endangered but really meaningful structure of the common life, the revolutionry from that of a dehumanizing world which must be overthrown if man is to gain his identity." [12] West elaborates this difference again in the following fashion: "We are confronted . . . with a basic conflict of unvarnished human experience: on the one side the experience of a precious humanity which must be secured and cultivated in an alien world, on the other the experience of an intolerable inhumanity imposed by a system which must be overthrown in order that man may find himself again." [13]

West sees the conference at Geneva as a microcosm of two forces at work in the contemporary world, each one committed to a new order of human existence, but each differing from the other in its experience of the world and therefore of what is required for that new order. For the one, the hope of a new day stands in drastic contradiction to previous and present experiences. For the other, the hope for, and vision of, a new day has clear continuities within, as well as contradictions of, previous and current experiences.

But one notes immediately that the stances represented by the technologists and the revolutionaries are not unique twentieth-century moods and motivations. There is a clear continuity between the revolutionaries and those who have seen Christ as opposing the dominant culture. Their experience is that of the apocalyptic crisis. And there is an echo in the technologists' experience with those who have sought to retain a tension between Christ and culture. They may be said to represent the Great Master Plan Christians.

In linking together the historical studies of Niebuhr and Reuther with West's observations about the contemporary scene, we illustrate divergent but continuing responses within the Christian community to what is required for the realization of the eschatological hope. What is divergent are fundamentally different religio-cultural experiences, and from those differences emerge disparate stances toward what is operationally required for the peaceable city. Disagreements and conflicts about social policies to be pursued reflect different religio-cultural locations.

We will now focus on two such approaches. One I shall identify as the approach of all those whose experience stands in radical contradiction to their eschatological hope. This is the apocalyptic approach. The second approach gathers together all those whose cultural experience is one of both continuity and discontinuity with their expected eschatological hope. This is the reformist approach. These two labels are not intended to be evaluative in any way, despite what might be inferred from our discussion in the last chapter. Indeed, the two approaches might be better seen as interpretive devices. Also, we must not assume that one approach is necessarily totally exclusive of the other. They are differing emphases, not exclusive stances. As heuristic devices they are designed to assist in understanding the current scene and in interpreting what is going on consciously and unconsciously in the disagreement and conflict centering on what type of social policy is required for a peaceable city.

One could illustrate these two approaches by reference to the worldwide context of rich and poor nations. But the range of the problem is too vast and unfamiliar to serve our purposes at this point, though we shall return to that issue in the concluding chapter.

We turn to the experience of the United States in recent years to illustrate the fundamental contradiction between the eschatological hope and the present experience. These illustrations are not drawn from the narrow range of "religious" or ecclesiastical activity. Rather, as Reuther suggests, the structure of the apocalyptic and reformist experiences is decipherable in the human enterprise itself.

Deprivation, oppression, and alienation are the breeding grounds for the apocalyptic approach. Apocalypticism is always one giant step away from the world of everyday, where men often traffic casually in inhumanity. Yet the apocalyptic mood intensifies during certain periods of history. It becomes a viable option not just for visions but for activity, not just for isolated individuals but for groups, when what Arthur Schlesinger has called the "thin membrane of civility" that holds a people together undergoes severe stresses and strains. No nation and no people are exempt from the conditions that provoke an apocalyptic approach to social reality.

Indeed, one message that has massaged the United States in recent years is that an apocalyptic approach is a natural and viable option for many of its residents. Those so minded announce that this is a nation "sick unto death." It is a land where only destruction is a suitable antidote to its toxic conditions.

That apocalyptic mood does not exist apart from objective conditions. Thus, to understand the mood one must examine the structural, experiential conditions that provide its source. For it is the dilemmas and malfunctionings of the society that weigh upon the apocalypticists' spirits with increasing potency. A mood, we recall, has its source in some congery of external circumstances. My proposition is that the apocalyptic mood flows from and reflects grave societal malfunctionings, the consequences of which impinge immediately upon persons.

One way of indicating the societal malfunction is to describe the period as one that may be characterized as afflicted by a pathology of institutions. Institutions are patterns of common activity that function across time and that are supposed to meet human needs. Institutions are those skeletons that tie our common lives together and enable the various parts of the body to be held together. To say that the time is one of a pathology of institutions is to suggest the presence of institutions that do not function to provide for the health of the whole body politic.

On what grounds is such a judgment made? We can only rehearse here familiar dichotomies between intended functions and actual delivery for several crucial institutions in America.

First, economic institutions are to provide for the production and distribution of material goods among the social body in an equitable fashion. In one sense the American economic system is one of undoubted success. It is a system that had led to affluence for most. But its failures are also obvious. Using conservative figures, twenty million persons still fall below the established poverty level in this country. Malnutrition and hunger are rampant in city and countryside. An inflationary spiral has recently robbed the lower middle class and those on set incomes of real earnings, making them suspicious and fearful of the future. The unemployed or marginally employed, those least able to afford it, pay the heaviest costs of cooling the economy. The conclusion? For large numbers the economic institutions have not provided for the production and distribution of goods on an equitable basis. To many the economic system looms as a servant of privilege, not justice. The institutional contradiction between purpose and actual delivery is clear. It is experientially clear to those who remain impoverished, assaulted by the advertisements of success and the reality of an impoverished existence.

Second, political institutions are ways by which governments of, by, and for the people become viable. Yet for many, the parties which are the brokers and the agents of political power are more like foreign potentates than personal spokesmen. Their selection of candidates for office appears as arbitrary. Their accountability to a broad range of the citizenry seems remote. Their indifference to those on the margins of society is highlighted by their apparent catering to those occupying the seats of power and prestige. The Democratic National Convention of 1968 was the symbolic, and for many symptomatic, occurrence that dramatized an elitist control over political choices, as well as the inability of the political system to grapple with deep-seated issues, especially the Vietnam War. Indeed, the military engagement in Vietnam threatened to make war not the extension of political activity, as it had traditionally been defined, but its overextension and therefore the destroyer of politics itself. An ever present American cynicism about, and suspicion of, political activity thus has recently blossomed into an outright hostility toward, and an alienation from, the political processes. The disjunction between government of, by, and for the people as a stated commitment and the actual functioning of political institutions left its mark upon the people.

Third, the educational institutions of the society have as their purpose the provision of both humanizing and technical knowledge. The intent is to equip all the citizenry to play a full role in the drama of national life. Yet the reading scores of major metropolitan public school systems are hard evidence of the failure of such systems to provide even the technical knowledge requisite for participation in a high-technology culture. Further, the low percentage of blacks in the college population, despite intensive recruiting programs by many schools, indicates the failure of the educational institutions at all levels to provide for all. The disproportionate amounts of money available for public education in affluent suburban areas when compared with urban school systems document the inequitable opportunity afforded students. The implication of major universities in the military-industrial complex convinces many students of the corruption of higher education. The experience of thousands, if not millions, is the failure of the educational systems to fulfill their stated purposes.

We could cite other institutional failures. The system of delivery of health services is clearly inadequate. There is general agreement that the welfare system is a colossal failure. The charge of racism is justly hurled as a dehumanizing dimension of all institutions, and is documented in job placement, attitudinal responses to blacks, and advancement opportunities. The environmental pollution of air, water, and earth testifies to governmental and industrial institutions putting their own limited interests above those of the general welfare. And the presence of crisis administrative styles throughout the institutional order drains energies and creativity.

The thesis recalled by the assertions above is a familiar one. The dominant institutions of the American society are not functioning as they ought, either singly or together. They are deemed not responsive to the full range of their constituencies' legitimate needs and desires.

What is new is the emergence into public awareness of an apocalyptic approach to this pathology. The carriers of this approach have been a varied group, for in a period of such extremities many persons experienced simultaneously heightened concern, frustration, victimization, and failure. They were those about whom Joseph Bensman commented: "In every period of historical crisis there are groups, occupations and classes who are 'accidentally' located in the nutcrackers of history. Such groups experience in extreme form all the cross-pressures, tensions, and contradictions of a society in the process of tearing itself apart." In a problematic time, when the institutional pathology spreads its effects throughout the social system, the apocalyptic approach storms out of private and secluded locations, for example, pentecostal religious communities, and takes up a public stance. It identifies the whole system as evil and seeks a dramatic and instantaneous alteration in the social order.

Who are the groups that carry this apocalyptic approach? They are those who are oppressed, either "accidentally" or consciously, by the society. They are the victims infected by the institutional pathology. They are as well the alienated, those for whom the institutional patterns are more psychically than physically oppressive personally. The former group lives on the outskirts of the dominant institutions and suffers from their effects. The latter participates in the dominant institutions but is repelled by them.

Within every society there is a wide spectrum of groups representing diverse conditions and experiences. The following chart is suggestive of the diversity in the land and for locating those for whom the apocalyptic approach is a lively experience.

Victims	Alienated	Achievers	Victors
Minority groups: Blacks, Browns, Indians	Radical students	Professionals: Labor Union Members White Collar Workers Civil Service	Elitist leaders, in all areas
Economically deprived: often the above, plus long-term welfare residents, the geographically determined poor			
Unskilled or de-skilled			
etc.			

As with any spectrum, this one has no clear breaking points between the groups. They blend at the edges into one another, and there is even some jumping of categories. For example, the elitist leaders may feel at times alienated.

The "American Dream" has suggested that through individual or group effort one would move toward the Victor side of the chart. "A chicken in every pot." "A car in every garage." "Every man a millionaire." These popular slogans stated the expectation. It was a dream that assumed that institutional arrangements such as free land, the public education system, an expanding and dynamic economy, and an open political process would facilitate such movement for all. What has actually occurred, however, is that for various reasons, the institutional mechanisms have not had an appropriate "fit" with the material and psychic needs of a large minority of this population. Their needs have not been met adequately for years. They have been victimized by the social order. Their experience of frustration and oppression is of long duration.

Thus, from among the victims, the oppressed, the powerless, there arises the apocalyptic mood and approach, the sense of the system as totally evil, the need for a complete change striking responsive chords among those linked by a common condition. Revolution becomes a serious call, for it seems the only social policy that can provide for the radical change required. The nature of the revolution advocated will vary widely. But the call for a dramatic intervention in the resident kingdom of evil is given credence by the experience of the victims.

The oppressed have been joined in this mood and approach in recent years by some of the middle-class student population. While not victimized physically, they are alienated. The sources of this alienation are multiple. One is the threat of "the bomb." As George Wald, Nobel Prize winner and professor of biology at Harvard University, put it, "I think I know what is bothering the students. I think what we are up against is a generation that is by no means sure that it has a future." He then went on to add as another source of that malaise the population explosion. We could add the environmental crisis. The point is that the apocalyptic approach lodges in students who consciously and unconsciously fear that there is both literally and figuratively no future prospect in the way the world in general and their country in particular are going. A complete change is required.

But the sense of threat is not the only detonator of the apocalyptic approach among students. There is the experience of hope that stands in contradiction to current experience as well. This student generation is among the first to have a lively sense of being a member of one-world, of one world not divided between the superior and the inferior, but one world of common humanity, with common human problems and prospects. That sense, we would say better that experience that has been fostered by television and travel, clashes with what appear to be and are the parochial self-interests of one nation. Theirs is a vision of a co-humanity that is so intoxicating that, when joined with a recognition of the oppression visited upon minority groups here and abroad by their forebears and contemporaries, it incites a call to an absolute negation of the current systems of evil.

Referring again to our chart, we note that what is new on the spectrum is the rise of the alienated as a social group, separate from, but allied in some of their interests with, the oppressed. They, like the victims, suffer under the "system." They despair of its possibility of delivering on its promises. They respond with an apocalyptic approach.

For the apocalypticists, whether victims or alienated, there is a compelling vision that starkly contradicts what is. It impels them toward a polarization of social reality into the good and the evil. What is required is an immediate change in the structural arrangements of the present order, the exorcism of evil by the establishment of institutions of a completely different order than are present. If that change requires overt violence, then such violent tactics may be legitimately employed. Or, if the legitimacy of violence is denied, there must be developed other tactics that are aggressive and assertive of a new order.

For the apocalyptic approach, revolution summarizes the social policy advocated. This term, while having little precise content for many, signals a radical change in all the institutional systems, a change that should be introduced immediately and totally. There is no time for incremental change of a gradual sort. There is too much suffering now to warrant any further delay. Now is the time when the system must be overthrown. The call to revolution is an anguished wail sounded by those victimized by the pathology of institutions. Its strategy is confrontation and open conflict, "ruthless honesty" and "uncompromising activity." Its excesses are functions of its drive to divide the world into the good and the evil, sweeping ambiguity under the rug of necessity. But the apocalyptic approach bears a vivid expectation, not of a better, but of a new day that will soon dawn. The crises and the chaos are surely signs of the end of the old, evil, and tottering system, the imminent collapse of which will usher in a new age. This is the hope beyond hope of the apocalyptic approach. It is the expectation of a peaceable city beyond the chaos of the present.

Not all gripped by the apocalyptic experience engage in activistic behavior. Another alternative is withdrawal into privatism or limited groups. This approach signifies a search for a center of meaning within limited circles of families and/or friends. Such a withdrawal from the world may be practiced within paneled dens of suburban homes or within makeshift quarters of New Mexico communes, where a new consciousness is sought and stimulated. Wherever it occurs, whatever its geographical location, the withdrawal from the public sphere may be interpreted as a sign of despair over the "system's" delivering on its promised goals and ideals. This separation leaves things within the social order to continue on an assumed downward spiral into destruction.

The apocalyptic approach assumes the necessity for a total destruction of the present evil age. Some await the impending holocaust. Others seek to detonate it. But the social policy is one of revolution. The experience out of which this social policy emerges is that of oppression and alienation.

The second experience of the eschatological hope leads to a reformist approach. Those who are drawn toward this pole share in the benefits, influence, and power of the established system. Their experiences of its successes overbalances their recognition of its defects. Or at least they have sufficient expectation of its delivery of advantages that it is not counted as "all bad."

The reformist does not deny the injustices rampant within, and perpetrated by, the current institutions of the land. But he does not diagnose their condition as necessarily malignant. The pathology is one that can be cured. Of course surgery may be and is often called for. The infectious viruses of selfishness, hypocrisy, racism, and greed must be excised from their institutional locations. The institutions of society, whether educational, political, economic, or social, must be altered to be more responsive to the needs of all the people. The societal system must be reordered to extend its benefits and to alter its processes of participation. But the expectation is that the reordering can occur and remedy the problems as one works in and through the system and its various subsystems.

For the reformist the signs of success and achievement toward a more humane order are evidence of the overall system's openness for transformation. More employment opportunities for members of minority groups, more integrated schools, more adequate welfare benefits, the "winding down" of armed warfare in Southeast Asia, more money legislated for pollution control, the slightest sign of an advance in worldwide disarmament agreements, more straightforward ecclesiastical resolutions on social issues—all these and more, taken together or singly, re-enforce the already basically positive experience of the reformist. These victories confirm what he wants to believe—that orderly social change is possible through committed activity. These events empower him to seek other alterations. They are not evidences of "tokenism" but are evidential tokens of a better future. They affirm his past and present and provide hope for the future.

The reformist mood varies between "pessimistic hope" and buoyant optimism. But the experience that lies at its root is a deeply felt sense of both continuities and contradictions between the eschatological hope and the current condition and experience. The reformists are drawn mainly, though not exclusively, from the side of the achievers or victors.

In describing the reformists' approach, I have had occasion to use the term "more" as descriptive of their intentions and expectations. That is an accurate term to indicate the reformist stance. But "more" encompasses both quantitative and qualitative meanings. It may, of course, mean simply the extension of what already is available, though in a limited fashion, as in "more" welfare benefits. But it may also mean a qualitative change. Thus, making more power available to ordinary members of a political party instead of concentrating it in the hands of an elite means the inversion of a system from an aristocratic elitism to a democratic order. Or, the proposal of "more" welfare benefits may mean not only added allowances but a completely different system of providing a basic income to all citizens, as in a guaranteed annual income. "More" as it has been used here is both a quantitative and qualitative term. Indeed, it is the qualitative component of the reformists' approach that sets them apart from the Christ-of-culture perspective, or from that of the limited pragmatic style.

In tactics, the reformist by temperament and by conviction deplores confrontation and conflict. He combats a polarization strategy. Further, the reformist is persuaded of the inability and inaccuracy of dividing the world into good and evil in an absolute fashion. He is persuaded of the ambiguities of all life, both that of the institutional world and of human nature. He is suspicious of any scheme that promises a radically new day or new person. Yet at the same time that the reformist disbelieves in shattering established practices and institutions, he also is convinced that, if they continue in their petrified and dehumanizing form, they and all they involve surely must perish. What then is his operational model for formulating and effecting social policies that will contribute to a peaceable city?

The reformist adopts an operational model for *shalom* that assumes the multiformity of social existence, the pliability of systems to change, and the ability to elicit a wide range of cooperative support for particular reforming movements within the social order. The reformist isolates out of the complexity of the social order particular issues and concerns that, while interlocked with other issues, have their own immediate discreteness. These are issues that press upon life, indicating a severe deformation of humanity and/or a great promise for a more humane and just order. The reformist presupposes that there are no simple or single answers to such issues. There are only complex and multiple answers that must be given in chorus to a broad range of social problems and issues. But these answers will not be given in a single and dramatic converting action. They will be given only in a continued interaction that stretches out into the future and that operates on a broad front in the present.

The reformist approach thus has an operational model that seeks to identify and isolate particular issues and to contribute to the reordering of life by dealing with them. The reformist focuses his activity on changes within the subsystems, rather than on the system as a whole. His pragmatic activity isolates particular and limited concerns. But it is broadly pragmatic in that it acknowledges the connectedness of life and the need to take into account the web of life as well as its separate strands. It as well acknowledges the crucial role of a vision of life that can enable men to envision the future in terms of potentialities.

Thus, instead of a polarization model that seeks to draw lines between the good and the evil on more or less predetermined lines, the reformist mood and motivation have many poles which draw the attention and commitment of diverse persons and groups. The poles are particular issues which impinge for various reasons upon the consciences, visions, and interests of different people. For example, disarmament, race, and economic justice are three poles that attract and merit attention in a movement toward a peaceable city. But even these are abstractions until they are broken down into concrete alternative policy proposals that can arouse and focus activity. They also are interrelated, or ought to be seen as such.

The reformist approach expects and is committed to the proposition that discrete issues can attract support from people of diverse commitments and backgrounds. A welfare reform policy may enlist not only the welfare recipients as its base line and directing group, but also the middle class of both a so-called conservative and liberal bent. Or a campaign against an anti-ballistic missiles system may recruit not only scientists and professionals, but also students, politicians, minority groups, and suburban housewives.

In such an operational model there remain conflict and contention. Those are inevitable in *shalom* making. But there is no absolute conflict. It is conflict about specific goals and policies and the requisite resources required for such. There is still frustration, but it is not a diffuse sense of impotence. Frustration is itself tied down to a specific location where there may well be success as well as failure, fulfillment as well as despair. Struggle centers around concrete human needs and concerns, always with the goal of altering institutions to make them more humane.

The reformist approach springs out of a sense both of contradiction and continuity between what is hoped for and what is currently present. It presumes a sense of urgency about issues, as well as a serious and disciplined commitment to change. It assumes complementarity of activity on the part of different persons and groups. It involves an active no-saying to whatever harms persons, and an active yes-saying to all that promises to contribute to human fulfillment. And all this is embedded in decisions informed by careful and sensitive analysis of the contemporary scene.

We have looked briefly at two approaches to *shalom* making that are shaped by divergent cultural experiences. We must be careful to realize that both are subject to delusions. The apocalypticist as the bearer and sufferer of the acute crisis experience is apt to misjudge or not bother to count the limits of the possible. Because he is experientially convinced that he has little to lose and much to gain, he may exaggerate for himself and for others their actual historical prospects. Such exaggeration is of course reminiscent of those prophets whose expectations outran the limits of popular response. The apocalypticist is often the bearer of a tragic gift, a gift in opening up radical new vistas for understanding and responding to life, but tragic in that the gift is rejected by the dominant body.

On the other hand, the reformist is tempted to delude himself into identifying his own location and proposed policies with "all that is possible." He is apt to hold too tightly the reins of social change, exercising power and influence that will not recognize his own complicity in inhumanity. His own sense of inevitable ambiguity may dull him to the necessity to make discriminating judgments about better and worse. At his worst he is apt to be stampeded by fear and self-interest into the arms of those who identify the present with *shalom*. If that occurs, every activity that is different or unusual begins to loom as a portent of impending chaos, calling forth a sympathy for tyranny and repression. But such a response is no longer "reformist." For the reformist approach embraces change and seeks to direct it, so that a new qualitative pattern of life emerges. In doing so it accepts compromise, but guards against its tendency to compromise too soon, protecting its own interests.

The apocalypticist and the the reformist—two approaches to social reality present in the land and in the world today. But they are really themselves two poles representing differing moods, motivations, and operational models for guiding social change toward the peaceable city. They are poles between which those committed to *shalom* may move. Indeed, it appears likely that the experience of *shalom* as standing in a contradictory relation to the present assumes an apocalyptic dimension for all at some point in their historic pilgrimage, while at other times the reformist dimension is primary. The polar relation does not assume an exclusive location for the self or the group at all times. Even as cultural experiences shape the response to *shalom* making initially, so the alteration of cultural experiences may call forth new responses. In fact at the operational level the self who is single-minded in his commitment to *shalom* may be double-minded about what is required within a particular socio-cultural scheme. Thus, the mood of apocalyptic crisis that grips a person or group and urges dramatic and absolute action may be tempered by an analysis of power relations and possibilities within a system. An apocalyptic mood and motivation may yield to a reformist operational model toward social change. A similar interplay could occur for the reformist, where he may come to believe, for example, that a confrontation technique is required for change.

However, differing locations within the cultural experience predispose persons and groups toward different forms of activity. Yet the apocalypticist and the reformer, individually and corporately, require each other, though each is clearly tempted to identify the other as an outright opponent. If such an identification occurs, the common commitment to *shalom* is eclipsed, and energies and resources are expended not on the formulation and enactment of social policies that are on the trail of *shalom*, but on intramural feuding and hostility.

It is evident that the experience of most churches and churchmen in America is, as West has indicated, that of persons who start from "the experience of an endangered but really meaningful structure of the common life." Thus it is no surprise that their primary style of *shalom* making is reformist. What is necessary is that this be recognized, that its experiential rootage be acknowledged, and that its relativity and potential dangers and delusions be admitted, while its prospects and possibilities are exploited.

The reformist approach, further, must understand that it needs its own sensitivity to be refreshed and stimulated by those gripped by the experience of the apocalyptic crisis. Thus there is a requirement for those whose experience is primarily that of "power, possession, and confidence" to align themselves with the victims of the world, to hear out the alienated, and to work out new policies with the victims and the alienated. These new policies must expose and deal with the root problems as they are codefined by all parties. Only such a positive and dynamic relationship between those who are commonly committed to *shalom* can fuse visions and hurts and power in such a way that there can be social policies that are authentic to the presence and absence and mutual promise of *shalom*. Such a task involves sharing not only dreams and hopes, but experiences. For as it is in the root experiences that the divergence between the two poles may be found, so any cooperation must discover grounds for common experiences that will permit and engender communication and some degree of mutuality. Perhaps we could say somewhat simplistically that the discovery of a common life in a peaceable city in the future depends upon a common search now for those social policies that will lead to that city.

This call for a common search by those whose experience is drastically different may sound naïve, perhaps even absurd. But such is a requirement for those who confess that "He is our peace," and who not only look forward to the peaceable city but also seek to pre-enact it. Such a common search does not mandate agreement about what policies are to be pursued, though such would be hoped for. Nor does it deny the certain presence of tension and conflict. But it does promise a clearer self-understanding by all and a growing sense of humanness. The process of interaction between apocalypticist and reformer clarifies self- and other-understanding. George Herbert Mead has described how the self comes to consciousness of itself as he is required to think and visualize himself through the eyes and actions of others. The baby comes to its own self-image as that image is mediated by persons in the family. So it is with groups. They come to self-consciousness over against other groups. As Peter Worsley has put it, "Consciousness of self . . . arises out of this process of opposition and distinction. The *kinds* of opposition, however, are constantly shifting; new ranges of consciousness and belongingness emerge, and old identifications lose their significance." [14] New understandings and therefore new policies are dependent on such interaction.

In emphasizing divergent experiences of *shalom* as contributing to disagreements about the nature of social policies required in the search for a peaceable city, I have been highlighting only one component that contributes to the struggle over adequate social policies. In doing so I have slighted the continuing importance for social policy formulation and implementation of empirical analysis of the conditions of life. The contribution of the social sciences, for example, to the social policy task cannot be overemphasized. These disciplines provide important data for estimating what can be done and what resources are required for accomplishing certain goals, as well as for evaluating the adequacy or inadequacy of programs.

Kenneth Underwood underscored this use of empirical information as vital for the social policy task. Quoting from an unidentified poet who claimed that "the highest test of a civilization is its sense of fact," he went on to extol the contribution that empirical investigation and findings could make to reordering life. He wrote:

One begins with the truth that is known about a particular situation, a real external part of the world, which dissatisfies or excites people either as a restraint on their humanness or as an offer of some hope to those involved. If the discussion begins with the introduction into public consciousness of what first outraged people, because it blocks hope for more meaning and significance to life, an important act of healing of the body politic has taken place. The act marks an end to private fantasies. Men and women are able consciously to look at what problems and realities they may be able to handle and no longer see the area as full of mystery. This reduces fear and hostility toward the situation under inquiry. The deeper a group probes the concrete realities of a situation, the more options for action can be envisioned.[15]

In emphasizing the cultural experience's impact on operational models for acting in the world, I did not intend to exclude the type of inquiry and information referred to above. I have done so, however, out of a conviction that the experiential location will inevitably shape even how one reads and uses "facts," or, for that matter, whether he will even consider them. If we are not self-conscious about where we are standing experientially when we are using information, then the information itself can easily be ignored or distorted.

"Blessed are the peacemakers!"

But the making of peace requires the discipleship of social policy, involving conflict and contention, as well as commitment and discipline. It involves projecting specific purposes and marshaling adequate power, all informed by the eschatological hope of *shalom*. It requires as well an operational model as to how one is to understand and respond to the social reality. One must be candid and wise in adopting such a model. Thus, an eschatological symbol requires a model for human activity if it, the symbol, is not to be victimized by naïveté or sentimentality. That model is itself influenced by the cultural experience of those who work out its contours. It is therefore clearly highly relative and provisional, penultimate, open itself to being broken apart by the judgment and grace of the God whose word comes in and through the trials and joys of the life lived in common with our fellow human beings. It comes particularly, however, through the cries and needs of the victims of the world.

In his novel *The Plague*, Albert Camus, a peacemaker, though not a Christian, had one of his characters describe the world as composed of pestilences and victims. The character says: "I grant we should add a third category: that of the true healers. But it's a hard fact one doesn't come across many of them, and anyhow it must be a hard vocation. That's why I decided to take, in every predicament, the victims' side, so as to reduce the damage done. Among them I can at least try to discover how one attains to the third category; in other words, to peace." [16]

In formulating social policy, Camus seems to be saying, for our purposes, people only learn how to be healers of the social order when they take the victims' side and let them be the prompters as to what it is that will make for the peace of wholeness, health, and security for all. That is a clear echo of the message of *shalom*.

Social policy that takes the side of the victims, and that takes into account the alienated, maps out the way to the peaceable city. Such social policy discipleship sets the world within a framework of promise not only symbolically but operationally as well.

Chapter V
Hope and Power:
Conditions for *Shalom*

Peacemaking requires interior moods and motivations and the external ordering of social life. To be gripped by the power of God is to be accorded a range of such interior gifts and to be impelled toward reordering social institutions. *Shalom* as a comprehensive symbol encompasses implications both for the self's personhood and for the objective social order.

The moods and motivations that accord with God's gift of and call to *shalom* are multiple. The ability of language balks before the richness. Nouns such as courage, faith, trust, peace, hope, security, loyalty, steadfastness, and love parade before the mind, attempting to reflect something of the glory of the coming of God to men and of men's response to that coming. In a similar fashion the requirements for reordering the social life are staggering in their breadth and complexity. Information, power, consent, analysis, organization, communication—all these and more are necessary for the achievement of social policies that are shaped by the peacemakers.

I shall enlist only two such terms as examples of the provisions that God makes for those who are aligned with his purposes. The first, hope, is what I have called earlier a mood and motivation. Hope is a persisting and powerful disposition or tendency of the self. As a mood it rests on a source, and as a motivation it tends toward an end. The second, power, is a necessary resource for the ordering of life.

These two, hope and power, do not stand alone in the panoply of provisions necessary for the Christian search for the peaceable city. They are chosen because they fit well with the symbol of *shalom* and with the task of social policy formulation. In treating the two separately, initially at least, I am not suggesting that the self in its attitudinal or dispositional character can be separated from the self in its involvement with others in the social sphere. It is one self. And hope and the exercise of power are two elements in the single self's response to God and neighbor. We shall first turn our attention to hope.

The Christian hopes. He hopes in God. The foundational source of this mood called hope, this persisting "set of the self" toward his environment, is the self's conviction about, and his commitment to, the God whom he has known through Jesus Christ. The relationship of hope is a function of having been gripped by the power of God. To hope is to be convinced that the ultimate source of all that is is both good and powerful. It is to be persuaded that the promises of God to Abraham, Isaac, and Moses, to David and the prophets, and to and through Jesus Christ are the promises upon which life can be based and which are authentically validated, though fragmentarily and episodically, in the self's own life. God as the source and power of *shalom* is the source of hope. Thus, as James M. Gustafson has noted, hope is always correlated with faith as trust in God.[1] Christian hope is, then, initially hope not in the self, nor in the neighbor, nor in any social schemes or plans. It is hope in God as the One who is the primary actor in the universe and whose acting is on behalf of his creation. This ground of hope provides the context and the relational framework for all of the Christian's other hopes.

Hope in God, Christians affirm, is a gift of God. It is the gift of his presence among us now and in the future, as it was present in Jesus Christ. The certainty of hope rests on a conviction about God.

As a motivation, Christian hope tends toward the end which it believes God is seeking. It moves the self out of the past and present and toward those conditions that reflect, approximate, or pre-enact the peaceable city. To hope in God correlates with a positive attitude toward the potentialities of the self's being and activity. For as hope in God, Christian hope reflects a belief that God has called the self and others to share in his work. Those who hope in God are agents of God's activity, coworkers with him, in the seeking of that justice and righteousness that make for peace. Thus, the self is motivated to act toward the end which God intends, with a firm expectation that his work is significant and productive, in positive correlation with God's own acting. Hope impels the self toward participation in shaping life. And active participation in reordering the world is a sign of the presence of hope as a mood and motivation. The late Professor Joseph Haroutunian put it this way, "We may not confuse the work of God with our work; but also, we may not separate them, for they are bound together by the Spirit." [2]

As hope in God, the transcendent sacred power, Christian hope points to a relationship that protects the self against two temptations. Christian hope is a barrier against both naïve optimism and corroding despair.

Naïve optimism expects the best possible outcome of all events. The optimist projects his plans, gathers his resources, and expects the best. He peers out upon the world through "rose-colored" glasses, greeting each occurrence with a broad smile. He plots his social policies anticipating nothing but success, as he has defined its composition. The utopian is the optimist par excellence.

But plans go awry. Failures occur. Betrayals intervene. Unexpected factors and movements insert themselves into the picture. What the optimist hoped for does not take place. A result is disappointment or cynicism. In the debilitating aftermath of failure or loss the optimist now knows better than to hope again. But the problem is not failure. The problem is that the source and object of the optimist's hope are too limited to withstand frustration or disappointment. The optimist hoped in himself and in an extension of himself—his plans, his resources, his group. Thus, for example, in designing and projecting the future, his own and his fellows', he thought he could control that future. He lacked a sense of its openness and his own limitations. On the other hand, Christian hope knows the future as in God's control. It is therefore an open future, both in terms of potential newness and in terms of frustration. Plans and projections are at most tentative and provisional. They are penultimate.

To hope in God is, thus, to be able to affirm that disappointment and defeat, the frustration and failure of one's best-laid plans, are cause for alarm. But such events are not destructive of the self's confidence and motivations. Hope in God is a persisting mood and motivation, undergirding the self despite failure and disappointment. To hope in God is to be able to recognize that the self moves forward always toward a future that he does not yet fully know and cannot fully control. That future may not develop as he would prefer. It may even seem in a problematic time to be more threatening than promising. But the ground of hope in God enables the self to expect God's purpose to be effected, no matter what happens. Hope clings to God, so that it persuades the self that, in the apostle Paul's words, "neither death, nor life, nor angels, nor principalities, nor things present, nor things to come, nor powers, nor height, nor depth, nor anything else in all creation, will be able to separate us from the love of God in Christ Jesus our Lord" (Rom. 8:38-39). Hope in God does not insure the self against disappointment. It does release him from naïve optimism. It also frees him from allowing disappointment to plunge over into despair.

Despair is a sin against God.[3] It is a negative relationship between the Christian and God. It is the dark side of hope. Despair is a relationship marked by a conviction that God is powerless in his goodness or else evil in his power. It is a mood of the absence or hostility of God.

Despair as a mood pervades the self. It corrodes any expectation that God will effect his purpose of *shalom*. It denies actively the possibility of a fruition of life for one's self or for one's neighbors. It envisions human prospects as bleak and dreary. Despair motivates the self not toward participation in the shaping of the peaceable city, but in indifference or opposition to any such activity. Despair, so understood, is an affirmation that one's own and one's neighbors' lives are useless, insignificant, lacking in ultimate meaning and direction. It may issue in disregard or denial of the neighbor. As a persisting mood and motivation it undercuts positive activity in the world, either of the self or of the neighbor.

Despair has many roots. Its exterior condition may be that of starvation, oppression, dehumanizing treatment, or any other one, or a combination of practices that disfigure human life. Out of such conditions Christian hope has often been expressed in purely otherworldly terms. But even that type of expression has testified indirectly and horribly to hope's power. Such a recognition warns the Christian and the church of the need to take great care when assigning responsibility for despair as a sin against God. It is not the victimized whose despair arises out of inhumane conditions that sin against God and who should therefore be upbraided for their response. It is that dominating community that has not believed the promise of *shalom* and has not had an active hope toward the peaceable city. That dominant and dominating community is guilty of the despair against God, denying the gifts and call of God.

Despair may be rooted in satiety as well as in oppression, or the absence of material well-being. The self who "has everything" may be gripped by a form of "worldly despair." For he has sought and gained what appeared to be fully satisfying. But he remains empty. He despairs of any fullness of life. The bright source and object of his hopes become as ashes. The writer of Ecclesiastes chronicled this mood.

> Vanity of vanities! All is vanity.
> What does man gain by all the toil
>   at which he toils under the sun? . . .
> All things are full of weariness;
>   a man cannot utter it;
> the eye is not satisfied with seeing,
>   nor the ear filled with hearing.
> What has been is what will be,
>   and what has been done is what will be done;
>   and there is nothing new under the sun.
>   (Eccles. 1:2, 3, 8, 9.)

Despair may result from misdirected hopes. It may be allied with the self's commitment to hopes which fail, to a relationship with an object, whether gold or power or knowledge, that betrays the richness of the self's destiny of life toward *shalom*. If so, despair is a sin against God, self, and the neighbor. It is a function of idolatry.

Hope in God is the antidote both to despair and to optimism. But to hope in the God who is known in Jesus Christ is to relate hope in God with hope *in, with,* and *for* the neighbor.

Christian hope is the expectation of the future which God intends. In characterizing that future as *shalom*, I have underscored that it is a social goal, a corporate enterprise. *Shalom* is peace with all God's creation. This understanding of the future of God and man and fellowman affirms a relationship of hope that binds together hope in God with the self's hoping in, with, and for the neighbor. To be given the gift of hope in God is to receive the gift of the neighbor as a source and object of our hopes. Hope is a mood and motivation that has a bearing not only on the ultimate. It embraces the penultimate as well.

Thus, even as we are to love God and the neighbor, so we are to hope, Christians maintain. The parallelism of love of God and neighbor is the pattern that applies to all the self's moods and motivations. The people .of Israel conjoined their hope in God with their hope for a promised land, a land flowing with milk and honey. To hope for a peaceable kingdom was to hope for a king who would rule with justice and righteousness. To give the blessing of peace to the neighbor was to will actively the neighbor's well-being. These hopes were correlated with, not antagonistic to, the hope in God, the expectation of the eschatological *shalom*. The future hope was linked with the realization of authentic human hopes in the present. It provided a canopy of splendor which sheltered and illumined the best human hopes as worthy of the attention and struggles of men. We can examine how the hope for *shalom* involves the Christian and the church in the search for a peaceable city only by emphasizing hope as *in, for,* and *with* the neighbor.

To hope in God is to hope *in* the neighbor. Hope in God is an entryway into the communion which exists through Christ between and among persons. In Christ, the hopeful self approaches the neighbor with the expectation that they shall be genuinely "brothers." "He is our peace, who has made us both one" (Eph. 2:14). Therefore, the hopeful self approaches each person anticipating a relationship that is mutually fulfilling. The assumption of the relationship is oneness, not hostility. For the Christian knows that his fulfillment and the fulfillment of the neighbor are interrelated. They are bound together by God. Thus, the one may and should contribute to the other's growth and development as a person. One hopes that in the relationship with any and all neighbors he may both give and receive that which makes for "peace and upbuilding" (Rom. 14:19). Thus to hope in the neighbor is to have a cast of mind or bearing toward him that looks for the self's fulfillment at his hands as well as to the self's contributing to his life. To hope *in* the neighbor is evidence of oneness in Christ. It is as well a preservative against pride, a representation of that genuine Christian humility that affirms that we need one another in order to be genuinely human.

Thus, no matter who the other is, the Christian hopes that he may enter into communion, be open to the other, and find their lives mutually enriched, that they may love one another. Hope then overcomes anxiety in the presence of the other and expels the self out of himself toward a common future. Without such hope the self would be immobilized as a fellowman.

This hope in the possibility of communion with the neighbor does not ultimately rest on that neighbor who confronts the self, on what he has done or not done in the past. It is set within the hope of life together, of *shalom*, promised by the God who has made himself known in Jesus Christ. It is therefore necessarily a sure hope, propelling the self simultaneously toward the neighbor and toward the self that he himself shall be. It rests on an anticipated future relationship, not on the relationship of the past. Thus, hope in the neighbor is a source of one's development as a person, a ground of growth, just as antithetically despair in the other is a source of the stunting of persons.

To recognize this ultimate setting for Christian hope in the neighbor is to be able to know that hope never fails. The person whom one approaches in hope may fail by turning away or misusing the occasion. He may betray the potentiality of the relationship. As Robert Johann has written, "We have all had the experience at one time or another of being let down by someone we trusted, someone in whom we had hoped. Christ himself knew what it is like to be betrayed. But this does not mean that we were wrong or foolish in hoping. It only means that the particular person on whom we relied has himself fallen short as a person, that he has declined the love which our trust in him made possible and has preferred to remain alone. Our hope was not a mistake, since it is, in a sense, something we owe to all. The mistake was his who freely chose to fail us and proved himself unreliable." [4]

To hope in the neighbor is genuinely to expect to receive goodness from the neighbor's hand. It is as well to expect to have one's gifts received by the neighbor. Hope energizes both giving and receiving. But the ground of that hope is lodged in a conviction that God is present in our midst to lead our hope to fruition. The self's vulnerability in hoping in the other, both friend and enemy, is preserved from the decay of despair and naïve optimism by the ground of hope, the power of God, for "he is our peace."

Not only does the Christian hope in the neighbor. He hopes *for* the neighbor. He hopes for the neighbor's well-being and well-doing. He identifies with the neighbor's hopes. Hope for the neighbor connects the future hope of eschatological peace with the present struggles of peoples seeking fruition. Hope generates love as the positive and effective seeking of the neighbor's good, whether he be near or distant, both geographically and psychically. Hope has therefore a bearing upon the concrete needs and expectations of the surrounding world. Indeed, the genuineness of Christian hope for, and commitment to, *shalom* is evidenced in its identification with the hopes of the neighbor.

It was the burden of the prophets to point out that the hollowness of the cry, "peace, peace," was caused by a neglect, whether benign or hostile makes no difference, of the concrete hopes of the people for food and clothing and justice. Authentic peace would mediate to men a fulfillment of their needs and expectations. Similarly the writer of the New Testament book of James puts the matter succinctly, "If a brother or sister is ill-clad and in lack of daily food, and one of you says to them, 'Go in peace, be warmed and filled,' without giving them the things needed for the body, what does it profit?" (James 2:15, 16.)

Today, in a period of history that has been characterized as a "revolution of rising expectations," it is just those rising expectations that have come into conflict with the often presumed hope that the Christian and the church held, i.e., a hope for life hereafter, "pie in the sky when you die by and by," etc. It was that misunderstanding of the hope of the church (a misunderstanding present both in and outside the church) that led Karl Marx and other critics to define the Christian faith's function as tranquilizing the self and the community. Eschatology, it was assumed, was a substitute for the realization of a just and satisfying life in the present.

But eschatology as a medium and a mode for understanding and acting in this world for the neighbors can affirm rather than deny the aspirations of this world. The *shalom* toward which Christians live is material well-being, health, and security for all. Therefore the human cries for food, shelter, and freedom and friendship are not foreign languages to the cry for *shalom*. They are a section of its vocabulary. The securing and enjoyment of such gifts are what it means to live together in a peaceable city. The search for, and the enjoyment of, such goods are magnets which should attract the hopeful activity of Christians and the church.

In discussing the misuse of eschatology and its need for reinterpretation within the church and world, Joseph Haroutunian summarized the temptation as well as the promise of the eschatological symbol. He wrote, "It is always easy to become fascinated with cosmic and 'fabulous' events which are to occur at the end of the world, and to lose both taste and courage to be concerned with lesser things which make the difference between honoring God and neglecting him. What is a cup of cold water compared with Noah's flood, or a piece of bread compared with the Banquet of the world to come! Yet we are done or undone as we offer or do not offer water to the thirsty and bread to the hungry. There is no faith or hope that can take the place of love, even though there is no love without both faith and hope." [5]

These penultimate needs and expectations of men—food, clothing, shelter, friendship, freedom—are authentic human hopes. Indeed one of the new realities of the current world is the anticipation taken root in the world that a materially and socially improved life is a right of all, not a luxury for the few. This plant has been nourished by the recognition that such a better form of life is genuinely within the scope of human potentialities. Starvation, oppression, bondage, suffering from material need or from political and social oppression—these are no longer perceived as inevitable fates. "Bread and dignity" are available to all.

Certainly multitudes have tasted this improved life only vicariously, through the media of radio or television, or through the agency of political promise. But the taste of a better life has whetted their appetite for actual deliverance from the systems of drudgery and inhumanity that have reigned. Those gripped by the experience of the apocalyptic crisis do not urge resignation. They call for revolution, and such a call is a sign that hope has replaced despair over ever changing what is. Revolutions are energized by a vivid expectation of, and aspiration for, a brighter day. Similarly the reformists focus on concrete changes to be made, changes that will provide for human needs. But both groups are moved by hope, and they are joined by those professing the Christian hope. Thus Christians hope for a better future for the neighbor.

This Christian hope for a better future dislodges the self from an overanxious and too-firm grip on the past and the present. Hope as a Christian virtue correlates with the future. Thus for Christian activity the future becomes as legitimate and as real a sphere of time as the past or present. The future as God's holds no ultimate threats. The newness that emerges out of the dynamism of life need not be met with initial or prolonged suspicion and hostility. Change and innovations, the emergent and emerging possibilities of life, the strangeness of new ways and languages and peoples—all these can be faced with the confident expectation that they are as surely in God's control and care as any previous ways or times or peoples. Thus, Christian hope embraces the emerging and unseen future with courage and love. Such a hopeful mood and motivation enable the self to live toward the future as promise, not threat. They dispose him to participate in shaping that future. They impel him to seek a peaceable city for the neighbors of the world.

Christian hope is hope *with* the neighbor. Hope's expectation of *shalom* as embracing all God's creation couples the self with all other persons in a mutual search for the peaceable city. The Christian hope is not a superior patron of the lesser hopes of other men. It is as a fellow yearner that the Christian and the church meet other persons and groups. This *hope with* keeps *hope for* from being paternalistic and self-serving. It also re-enforces the mutuality of life that was the brunt of our discussion about *hope in.* For *hope with* the neighbor interlocks the Christian with the neighbor, both other Christians and those not so called, in the struggle for a peaceable future. It associates the task of the formulation and implementation of social policy with a genuinely human task, in which none are barred from participation, indeed all are enrolled.

This hope with the neighbor involves as its correlative partner a renunciation of the world. But the renunciation is not a withdrawal from the world. It is a withdrawal of identification of God's purposes with any particular organization and practice of the received social order. It is a recognition by the Christian and the church of their need to withdraw any conscious or unconscious underwriting of their own position and privileges as necessarily equated with what God wills. This form of renunciation is particularly pertinent for those whose cultural experience has been primarily that of "possession, power, and confidence." It is a lever against self-satisfaction. It guards against renunciation as being trivial and token, as in "giving up meat" for Lent. This different shape of renunciation molded by the hope for *shalom* has been described by Johannes B. Metz in the following fashion: "Not a flight *out* of the world, but a flight *with* the world 'forward' is the fundamental dynamism of the Christian hope in its renunciation of the world. This renunciation is therefore a flight only out of that self-made world which masters its present and lives solely out of its present, and whose 'time is always here.' " [6] Such a form of renunciation "clears the decks" for being with the neighbor, even as his hopes impinge on the self's own standing and privileges and power.

In hoping with the neighbor, the Christian identifies with the legitimate aspirations of others. Christian hope thus activates persons and groups toward the realization of a more humane order of life. Such an emphasis on mutual support and struggle needs to be made again and again. But there is also another word which the Christian says in his engagements with his neighbors. Jürgen Moltmann has pointed to this "other word." "The Christian hope is directed . . . towards a new creation of all things by the God of the resurrection of Jesus Christ. It thereby opens a future outlook that embraces all things, including also death, and into this it can and must take the limited hopes of a renewal of life, stimulating them, relativizing them, giving them direction." The Christian hope takes up all the human hopes of men. But it puts them within a different framework. In doing so it provides a necessary word for all hopes. Moltmann continues: "It [the Christian hope] will destroy the *presumption* in these hopes of better human freedom, of successful life, of justice and dignity for our fellow men, of control of the possibilities of nature, because it does not find in these movements the salvation it awaits, because it refuses to let the entertaining and realizing of utopian ideas of this kind reconcile it with existence." [7]

In hoping with the neighbor Christian hope does not deny the legitimate nature of human hopes. It firmly supports the limited and penultimate hopes of persons, hopes for food and shelter and dignity. But it insists that even these goods can themselves become demonic, dehumanizing, sources of a new despair and/or bases for new oppressions. For in seeking the good things of life persons and groups may attain them, expecting to find ultimate satisfaction and fulfillment. Yet those very goods for which they rightly hoped may and do become powers in themselves. Their attainment can serve to isolate men from their neighbors, rather than knitting them together. Hopes realized may become alienating agents, so that those who have obtained dignity of position and power may deny the same prospects to their fellow human beings. Even the good hopes for which men strive may become sources of despair for themselves and others. The collapse of the Christian hope into any absolute identification with any single hope or cluster of human hopes is to rob the neighbor of what is necessary for authentic life. Christian hope as identification with the neighbor in his legitimate worldly hopes does not mean the identification of the fullness of the Christian message with any particular statement of penultimate hopes. We recall Bonhoeffer's warning about the identification of the ultimate and the penultimate.

In hoping with the neighbor, Christian hope identifies with the neighbor. But it is only as the good hopes of men are related to hope in the transcendent power of God who

is seeking the peaceable city that they are properly con-
textualized. Human hopes are then affirmed as legitimate,
but directed to their proper use—the building up of all the
neighbors. They are also set within a dynamic expectation
that is constantly unfolding, unwilling to define the fullness
of life in terms of any realized goal or social policy. *Shalom*
as an eschatological symbol exerts a pull on any and every
present, transforming it and breaking it open toward the
emerging future.

This ultimate word that the Christian and the church
utter in their hope with their neighbor is not for the benefit
of the church. It is for the well-being and well-doing of
their neighbors and themselves. It is a word said to themselves and to others. It cannot authentically be said until
and as the Christian and the church have demonstrated their
commitment to the realization of the good hopes which grip
the world and are so demonstrably needed. Otherwise the
word comes as gratuitous and often as self-serving. But the
ultimate word may legitimately be said by the Christian
and the church, especially by the main-line Christian groups
of the West. For it has been and is their past and immediate
experience that an abundance of food and shelter, of rich
clothing and well-financed social institutions, of power and
prestige, have not been for them the mediators of a peaceable city. These have as often promoted relationships of
hostility and separation, of limited well-being, as they have
been carriers of the *shalom* of material well-being, security,
and health for all. In the Christian community these hopes
too often displaced their hope in God. Thus they know
by experience that only as these hopes are set within the
context of hope in God's *shalom* do they contribute to a life
that is genuinely human, authentically one of peace.

We thus come full circle in our consideration of hope.

163

We began with hope in God, and then moved to hope in, for, and with the neighbor. Now we have emphasized how identification with human hopes leads inevitably to hope in God, at least for the Christian. Christian hope is hope in God and his intentions, in *shalom*. That ultimate hope affirms the creaturely hopes of all men, is open to them, identifies with them, but contextualizes all such hopes and their realization in terms of the future that is in God's hands and therefore *for* men. The Christian hope refuses to destroy the tension between the eschatological expectation and the actualization of present hopes. To do so would be a sin against both God and neighbor.

Hope as a persisting and powerful mood and motivation extends the self out into the historical future. It activates and mobilizes the self to participate in the present as a time filled by the promise and potentiality of newness. Hope does not deny or ignore the reality of struggle, suffering, and defeat. It engages the present with a realism about the continuing power of evil. But a realism of hope contextualizes the power of evil as subject to the power of God.

Christian hope is therefore not a flighty or fanciful attitude and stance toward life. It is lodged in a clarity about life illumined by the life, death, and resurrection of Jesus Christ. It is a part of the bundle of life that flows from his power. The apostle Paul, in his letter to the Romans, summarizes the interconnectedness of hope with other elements of the Christian life when he writes: "Therefore, since we are justified by faith, we have peace with God through our Lord Jesus Christ. Through him we have obtained access to this grace in which we stand, and we rejoice . . . in our sufferings, knowing that suffering produces endurance, and endurance produces character, and character produces hope, and hope does not disappoint us, because God's love has been poured into our hearts through the Holy Spirit which has been given to us." (Rom. 5:1-5.)

Hope is thus an active virtue. It exercises the self. One way in which it functions is in stimulating the self to utilize the resources available to reshape the world toward *shalom*. The frustration of hope often lies in the absence or inadequacy of the requisite resources. Moltmann is suggestive of this when he writes, "The pain of despair surely lies in the fact that a hope is there, but no way opens up toward its fulfillment. Thus the kindled hope turns against the one who hopes and consumes him." [8]

Hope's imperatives for the formulation and implementation of social policy require the marshaling of resources, if hope is not to turn into despair. Hope, we have contended, affirms that the true form of personal life is the community of *shalom*, the peaceable city. But, as we have noted above, hope does not sentimentalize or spiritualize that community. Christian hope acknowledges that the form of personal life as community is a force-field, a network of interactions and transactions between and among persons and groups. In such a force-field a crucial issue in the search for a peaceable city is the use and misuse of power. For power is a resource which hope recruits in its struggle toward *shalom*. Without power hope becomes an empty wish, an illusion, a bad hope that disfigures life.

In the recent American scene, perhaps no question has taxed the emotions and minds of persons more than that of power. A consciousness of the presence and absence of power, its use and misuse, its centrality for the self and for the reordering of society, has swept over the land. Slogans such as "Black Power," "Power to the People," "Brown Power," "Green Power," "Polish Power," and "Women's Power" have served to signal that the issues of power distribution and power use are basic ingredients of the contemporary scene. There has arisen a reconsideration of power as fundamental for the self's being and functioning. This has been accompanied by discussions about the social location of power and its consequent effects on persons. A consideration of power as a central resource for the contemporary search for a peaceable city requires a cursory examination of the social context out of which the cries for a re-examination of power and power relations have emerged.

What is the nature of this social context that has fostered a cry for reopening the question of power? It is multidimensional. But we will focus on one of those dimensions. This is the conviction on the part of many that they are victimized by the current power arrangements. They experience more their impotence than their power. Such an experience leads many to believe that they are more acted upon than acting, that they are as pawns in some great chess game, that they are lost within and dwarfed by the vast movements of the technological society and the giants of government, business, and labor.

If we define power as the ability of the self to act, individually and in concert with others, in a way that achieves the conditions that the actors deem desirable, then it is the absence of power that is experienced by many today. We can illustrate this sense of an absence of power by looking at various subjective statements that reveal personal moods. These moods are the result, however, of current social practices. Therefore our examination of the social context combines both moods and social locations for such moods. We begin with the former.

Studs Terkel has a peculiar gift for enabling people to verbalize the things they feel. His book *Division Street, America,* is a compilation of his interviews of persons from various walks of life. Terkel contends that in these interviews he has caged attitudes prevalent throughout the country. One of the recurring moods his tapes record is a malaise of the spirit. It is a mood of frustration, a feeling expressed by many that they are caught within a situation where their contribution to life about them extends from the minimal to the nonexistent. It is the mood of those who sense themselves submerged beneath an ongoing process of life. It is a mood of impotence, of absence of significant power.

One interview crystallizes this mood. It is with Miss Florence Scala, independent candidate for alderman of the First Ward in the city of Chicago, a ward noted for its alleged crime syndicate affiliations. In the election Miss Scala lost by a more than two-to-one margin, despite the assistance of numerous volunteers rallied from all over the metropolitan area. In the interview Miss Scala observed the following about the volunteers. "There were people from all over Chicago campaigning for me, some people I never saw before nor have I seen since. . . . They weren't always people I see eye to eye with . . . . I couldn't understand what it was in me they wanted to support. But there was something. I have a kind of sympathy for whatever it was that was frustrating them. I really do, because they felt themselves unable to count somewhere." [9]

It is the last statement that summarizes a dominant mood in the American scene. "They felt themselves unable to count somewhere."

This expressed feeling is one that joins with a general attitude recorded and documented as a part of the American scene. It is the sense of an absence of significant power for the self, either individually or with others. Scholars, dramatists, novelists, journalists, and many others have over the years described this mood. For example, social scientists and creative artists both have registered, while often lamenting, the absence of any sense of significant power in their work for those whose assembly line jobs required a repetitive and mechanical function. No one has denied the importance of such jobs being done well. But all have remarked on the way in which this kind of machine-tending depersonalizes the self, that is, reduces the self and the richness of his being by overemphasizing a limited function that he performs, one that requires little meaningful expression of his powers.

This type of analysis applies not only to workers on production lines. It is appropriate for increasing numbers of white-collar workers and professionals as well. One source of this mood is the vast size of organizational units in the high-technology culture. Another is the organizational principles which function to allocate tasks and assign responsibilities.

Chris Argyris, a student of organizations and their functioning, indicated in a popular article how industrial organizations attack humanness by robbing persons of their ability to act meaningfully. The fault lies in assumptions about human nature. Two principles dominate. Argyris defines them. "Work should be simplified and specialized so that it will be easier to plan, control and direct; and management should not be directly involved in producing the work." He continues by spelling out the personal implications of these principles. "From an employee's point of view this means that he is asked to be more passive than active, more submissive than responsible; to use his shallow, surface abilities and ignore his more complex and deeper abilities. Such conditions are better suited to the world of infants than adults." [10]

The application of such principles is not limited to the industrial sphere. Large-scale bureaucratic organization, whether it be political, economic, educational, religious, or social, operates on similar principles. Such an organization squeezes the self, restricting the range of its expression. As a result the self is given a message about himself by his location within organizations. It is that he is powerless both within the particular structure and also as an agent to affect the vast systems which shape his life.

As suggested earlier, there is a wide range of literature documenting this condition. It locates the mood of a sense of being "unable to count somewhere" in the "depersonalization" of the social order. By depersonalization is meant the organization of the social structures in such a way that the self is more of an object than a subject. The self's individuality is subordinated to systematizing processes, wherein the self has little or no space for the exertion of his powers in a way that he can see as making any significant difference for his fellowmen.

This sense of alienation from the exertion of significant power is a sense of alienation from one's self. For the self is an actor who is called, or so I have contended, to utilize his abilities on behalf of some desired condition, some purpose. To strip the self of purposeful acting is an attack upon his being. And this sense of alienation is not a disembodied feeling that can be cured by soothing words or banal denials. As a mood it is grounded within the pathology of institutions which we have discussed previously.

There are two qualifying points to insert in our discussion. One has to do with the perennial condition of the exercise of power. The second is a reference to the contemporary period.

First, in the perennial condition of the exercise of power,

the individual or the group is set within a context that affects what can be done. No person or group is devoid of surrounding influences when he or they act. The image of life as a force or power field reenforces such an understanding. The capacity for achieving desired ends is always a free exercise of power within a condition of limitation and counterforce. Theodore Sorensen in *Decision Making in the White House* describes how even the vaunted power of the presidency is blocked and conditioned by a plethora of pressures and forces. We all exist in a network of interactions and transactions of dynamic interrelationships, which have affected and do shape what we are able to do. The exercise of power is always a mixture of freedom and determinacy. That is a perennial condition for man. Such a recognition warns against absolutizing the present as one uniquely limiting of the exercise of power, whether by individuals or groups.

Second, there is a large body of literature analyzing the contemporary social order that is more sanguine about the place that individuals and groups have in achieving desired ends. This emphasis is important to balance the often exaggerated, sometimes manic, outcries against the dehumanizing and oppressive conditions of the high-technology culture. Indeed, such analyses are themselves antidotes for despair about the possibility of effecting social policies of a positive sort.

Nevertheless, the evidence of depersonalization as a continuing reality and threat to personhood, both for those within and without the dominant systems, cannot be ignored. The bias of *shalom* is in favor of those processes and procedures that empower rather than deprive selves. Those committed to peacemaking are advised to proceed on the assumption that there are genuine reasons for the widespread sense of frustration and anguish. Thus, I have chosen here to emphasize powerlessness, not because it is the only thing to be said about contemporary society, but because it is sufficiently documented by subjective statements and by objective examination to indicate a genuinely human problem, i.e., a stated issue that requires attention and remedy.

For our purposes, the problem of depersonalization can be defined as structural powerlessness. It is a problem of mood. But more fundamentally, it is a problem of the source of the mood, a problem of societal institutions that by their organization and vastness limit severely the self's exercise of power, his "ability to count." This is a threat to deprive the self of the possibility of participating in shaping the future in any significant fashion. It is the alienating from the self of a crucial element of his being, the exercise of his abilities and energies individually and with others toward desired ends. It is the absence of a condition that allows for and encourages the self individually and with others to experience what Kenneth Underwood called one of the most important things in a person's life, "being able to participate in shaping a corporate enterprise into becoming something important in the hopes and expectations of others."

Thus far, references have been to those persons and groups whose sense of powerlessness was related to a depersonalizing life experience within the dominant social institutions. There is another type of experience, of those who have been oppressed by the social order, the victims. Their experience of social impotence is rooted elsewhere.

Kenneth Clark reports some of the voices of the oppressed.

"A lot of times, when I'm working, I become as despondent as hell and I feel like crying. I'm not a man, none of us are men!

I don't own anything. I'm not a man enough to own a store; none of us are." Man, age about 30.

"I think there's a great lack of offensive direction and most of the adults have, more or less, succumbed to the situation and have decided, what the hell can I do? This is the attitude; that we can do nothing, so leave it alone. People think you're always going to be under pressure from the white man and he owns and runs everything, and we are so dependent on him that there's nothing I can do. This is the general impression I've gotten from most of the adults in Harlem." Girl, age 15.[11]

These are direct quotations from Harlem, New York City. But they express a mood present in many minority locations across the land. The mood is not the only one present. But it is a disposition that even more militant leaders and groups acknowledge as potent. It is a mood that rests on a condition of deprivation. One of the most salient features of the experienced deprivation is that of an absence of significant power. The oppressed, the victims, by definition, are deprived of the power to make decisions and to act in a way that effects desirable changes in their lives and in the larger society.

Kenneth Clark has argued that one of the salient features of the minority culture is its lack of power. This absence does not result from a character trait. It is the direct consequence of the disinherited's social location. Clark describes this as an institutionalization of powerlessness. By this he means that the usual forms and patterns that provide persons with an ability to exert control and direction over their own individual and corporate destinies are missing or, at best, only minimally present. For example, major economic institutions, banks, industrial plants, and retail outlets are owned and controlled by persons who are members of the dominant society, not the minority group. Political power is held by persons who are beholden to those outside the minority culture and often use what power they have for personal aggrandizement. Real estate is owned by absentee landlords. School policy is set by a school board that has little or no direct contact with the constituency. The religious institutions too often peddle escapism.

The social condition that is the source of the mood of despair is exclusion from institutions of power. People are enveloped by power units. But they, individually and corporately, lack the instruments required to alleviate their misery and to achieve purposive ends. In distinction from those discussed earlier who participate in the significant social institutions and who feel that their participation leaves little or no space for significant decision making, the oppressed lack significant participation in the institutions themselves. They experience powerlessness far more severely than those mentioned earlier. Its effects are more direct. The rawness of its consequences is not mollified by the insulation of creature comforts and avoidance possibilities open to the achievers.

Nevertheless, the pathology of institutions as depriving persons of significant power is a condition that unites the victims and the achievers. The type of analysis that assigns frustration in effective exercise of power only to the obviously deprived group is another example of the condescension and illusory rationalization of the majority. Again, this affirmation is not, of course, to deny the great differences in experience between the material and psychic conditions of the oppressed and those of the population who are included in the dominant institutions. Nor is it to be so naïve as to fail to recognize that the latter often use what power they have to maintain and even extend oppressive conditions for their brothers.

But the experience of powerlessness is widespread. It encompasses the victims and the achievers. It embraces the black, the brown, the poor of all colors and races, as well as large numbers of the urban and suburban middle class, the middle-class university students, and increasing numbers of the elderly. The frustration and fury they all experience is, to a degree at least, a function of their sense of alienation from the "most sensitive nerve in the American consciousness—the individual's desire for mastery over his own life and environment." [12] That is why the issue of who shall have power, and how and for what purposes it shall be exercised, has become such a central issue for the contemporary world.

The nature of the social context is not only the presence of a mood. It is an institutionalization of powerlessness, or of structural powerlessness. It is a state of a pathology of institutions. That is why the current search for personal meaning by those who are participants in impersonal and depersonalizing institutions links up with the search of the oppressed who have been left out of the institutions. Both call for new structures, new institutions. Both call for society's institutions to be reconstituted in such a way that all may participate as much as possible in and through them to attain desired ends.

There is today a widespread recognition that power in its distorted forms confronts persons with a disabling and dehumanizing context for life. It robs them of their humanity. There is also a conviction that power in its just forms, on the other hand, can and should provide persons with an enabling and humanizing context. If the problem of a sense of powerlessness is located within the recognition of an institutionalization of powerlessness, then energy must be directed toward the alteration of the social forms which provide for power distribution and exertion. Again, the strategy of the apocalypticist and the reformer as to what is required for new social policies will vary because of their differing experiences and analyses. What is common is the commitment to institutional provisions that will empower all persons. The rise of encounter groups, the new concern for leadership development, the middle-class emphases on democratizing political parties and educational systems may appear initially as distant strangers to the cries for "Black Power" or "Student Power." But they are in reality close cousins. The unity lies in the search for more adequate ways and forms for expressing one's humanness, one's power as a self and co-self, toward the future. More dramatically, an example of the similarity is the presence of overt violence, one source of which is the impotence persons feel in terms of their ability to "make a difference." As Rollo May has put it, "To inflict pain and torture at least proves that one can affect somebody." [13] And the violence of the streets is kin to the violence of conflict in middle-class families.

Hope and power go together. Institutions that do not enlist the power of their members and that are not accountable in their exercise of power to limiting forces breed despair. The institutionalization of powerlessness is the institutionalization of despair. On the other hand, institutions that invite and encourage genuine and significant participation are vehicles of hope. The institutionalization of participation is the institutionalization of hope.

Hope that does not promote power is an empty hope. It is an unwitting ally to its normal opponent, despair.

One of the continuing issues for Christians seeking the peaceable city today is whether or not they will come to an appreciation of the symbiotic relationship between Christian hope and power. To treat hope without providing for power is to raise false expectations and to be the parent of apathy and violence. But to treat power without attaching it to hope is either to legitimate the present power arrangements or else to leave power to random expression. Power must join with hope in the movement toward *shalom*.

There are then at least three considerations about power which must be reappropriated by Christians if they are to exercise a discipleship of social policy toward *shalom*. The first is the acceptance of the inevitability of the exercise of power by individuals and groups. The second is the cruciality of relating power to purpose. The third is the necessity of understanding power as an ordering resource. We shall look at each of these.

Power exertion is an inevitable part of the fabric of life. Paul Tillich has described this situation. "Every encounter, whether friendly or hostile, whether benevolent or indifferent, is in some way, unconsciously or consciously, a struggle of power with power." [14] What is required is a consciousness that life is a power field, a grid of power interactions. We affect others in one way or another. Clearly, the magnitude of power exerted by any one person or group is determined by various components, i.e., money, position, education, weapons, personality, etc. There is always an asymmetry of such relationships. This asymmetry is experienced as extreme and oppressive by many in various periods of history, of which ours is one. My point here is that there must be a consciousness that all life and all its tokens are engaged in power relations. One useful analogue for the self is that of a power unit in a power grid.

This consciousness of life as a power grid provides a way of asking questions about relationships. A fruitful inquiry is, "How do my power, my self, my group, my possessions, etc., affect others?" The recognition of the inevitability of power relationships provides an interpretive device that exposes new dimensions of relational patterns. All social groups, from the chance acquaintance through the family and up to the international community, are fit subjects for such an analysis. It is a type of analysis that often exposes gross, though unconscious, imbalances of power.

Further, such a recognition of life as a power grid argues against any interpretation of power as evil in itself. The question is not power or no power. Power is a reality to be acknowledged and dealt with, a reality with prospects and problems, laced with ethical ambiguity, but to be used or misused for or against what makes for peace. Power is endemic to interaction.

The second consideration is that power must be related to purpose. Christians affirm that the purpose of power is determined by the purpose of the sacred power, God. And that purpose we have symbolized as *shalom*. *Shalom* symbolizes the purpose of God's power and the purpose of human power relations. *Shalom* as a purposive symbol provides an evaluative instrument by which one takes the measure of current and future power relations. "Power to the people," for example, is a slogan used by various groups throughout history. The evaluative issue to be asked of all is the purpose of the power sought by the people.

The evaluation of power relations rests on some commitment to, and expectation of, what constitutes an authentic human community. Thus, Hannah Arendt has noted that what keeps a people together, what makes a city a city and not simply a collection of warring interests, is a mutual promise.[15] It is a promise to effectuate a certain kind of life together. Such a promise is a constituting agreement that may be written down in a constitution or that may develop over years of practice. That promise and its consequent actualization are crucial for the health of a people. For that promise is a statement of what makes an authentic human community. That promise enables a people to dispose of their future purposefully. If the promise is not kept, the people disintegrate. For it is the promise and its actualization that provide evaluative criteria for the present and the future disposition of life, for the use of power. For example, the United States Constitution is a promise of a certain form of life together, jointly entered into by the citizenry. It provides a purposive evaluative instrument by which to measure the use of power by the nation in both domestic and foreign relations.

For the Christian, promise and purpose are conjoined in *shalom*. The promise of God and the purpose of God are his universal reign in peace. The commitment of Christians and the church is toward the realization of that condition. They seek it now as a pre-enactment of that which lies ahead. Social policy formulation and implementation therefore seek a proper use and distribution of power in the here and now that will manifest a keeping of the promises of a peaceable city. The search is not just for an acceptance of power, but for a reordering of power relations so that all persons may exercise power and participate in an authentic human community. The search is for a context of power relations that may be enabling and humanizing, rather than disabling and dehumanizing. The search is for appropriate forms and institutions of a political, economic, and social sort, that will concretize hope by engaging the creative powers of all people. It is a search for institutions of peace. These then become signs of the authenticity of the promise.

The particular social implications for a reordering of power relations depend upon an evaluation of every present situation. One implication has been a necessity of balancing

and limiting powers that men exercise. Because God is absolute power, no man can attain or should seek such. But
even the principle of limitation of power can be misused.
H. Richard Niebuhr observed, "The principle of limitation
of power was subject to abuse, of course, in the interest of
whatever power happened to be in control." [16] Those in
power always want to limit others' power! The clear requirement for the present day is a reordering of power relations,
providing power for the powerless, balancing the asymmetry
of relationships. The promise and purpose of *shalom* can
provide an evaluative context for any particular consideration of power relations.

Power as an ordering resource is essential for effecting
social policy that coheres with *shalom*. That is my third
point. But *shalom* as a symbol of the eschatological future
to which God calls his creation suggests a particular understanding of power and order. We recall that Augustine, for
example, defined peace as a tranquillity of order. Order has
come to mean for many a static system in which power
relations are rigid. But the order of *shalom* in displacing
the self's primary orientation from the past and present toward the future provides a different perspective on order.
For order, then, is not so much that which *is*, or that which
has been. It is rather that which is to be. Power is referred
therefore to the function of ordering life forward toward
a peaceable city, not in preserving the present order. Power
has an ordering task, and it is exercised well when it is
engaged in the dynamic process of ordering life toward the
future. The assumption of peacemakers is that the present
is disordered, that *shalom* requires ordering, and that the
only ultimate order is eschatological.

This ordering of life toward the future involves power as a
resource correlated with hope. But while hope refers to an

interior mood and motivation, power directs the attention of the self and of groups outward, toward a reformulation of the conditions of life together, toward new and more equitable power relations. Power involves various agents, individuals and corporate bodies. But in the formulation of social policy, corporate bodies are essential. The exercise of corporate power, whether by political parties, business and industry, or religious institutions, is crucial for the reordering of the common life. Without embracing the positive role of corporate power exercise, the Christian and the church resign from effective discipleship in the world.

But embracing the exercise of power in the modern world as a task of being peacemakers sets the final stamp upon the recognition of conflict as an ongoing component of discipleship. In the search for a peaceable city there is no exile of contention and struggle. There *is* a struggle to locate conflicts within structures that humanize them by limiting their proportions and transforming their intentions. The individual and the group are, however, "called to do battle: there is no advance without it. If he [they] is also called to peace, it is because peace is not a state but a process, not just a matter of avoiding conflicts but of keeping our conflicts constructive." [17]

Hope and power are conjoined in the discipleship of social policy toward *shalom*. They are not only ingredients provided and required. But without them there is an eclipse of faithfulness. For both are legitimate not in themselves, but as correlated with the promises and power of God.

One name for the power of God granted in and through Jesus Christ is reconciliation. To be reconciled to God is to be given the power to overcome barriers and to provide for just forms of power for all.

Another name we give to the power of God is Incarnation.

One interpretation of the Incarnation is that of the presence of One who decided and acted under the conditions of humanity toward *shalom* in such a way that from his life, death, and resurrection there sprang up an institutionalization of hope, which we call the church. The church then is an extension of the Incarnation as it decides and acts with others to move men from powerlessness to power, from despair to hope, but not to one without the other. How the church may do so is our final consideration.

Chapter VI
The Church and *Shalom*

The church is a body of people who are gripped by and seek *shalom*. Christians consciously confess that their experience of, and search for, a peaceable city has been crucially shaped by Jesus Christ. They are aware that their witness to God's power and purpose is often distorted and conflicting, self-serving and limited in its scope. Like the people of Israel of old, they often witness to God's peace only negatively, so that they themselves must be admonished as denying those things that make for the fruition of life. Nevertheless, they define their being and function with reference to their understanding of God's intentions and activities. They seek to image his work of peacemaking.

The term church has, of course, many referents. It is used most commonly to refer to the building where people gather together for worship, teaching, and service. It is also applied to the body of Christian people who are scattered abroad in their various roles and functions. The term church may mean for others a mystical body, one whose contours must remain unmarked lest God's presence be identified with certain types of experiences or with certain groups and practices. For still others the church designates all those people who are engaging in the works of love, no matter what their own self-confession or protestation may be. The church is typified as well as the collection of God's chosen, the holy nation, the realization of the kingdom of God in miniature within space and time. Lest we forget, for some the term church signifies a repressive and hostile body that is an enemy to legitimate human aspirations and needs, whose power is aligned with archaic and oppressive interests.

I am using the term church in a limited sense. By church, I mean a human community that confesses Jesus Christ as Lord and seeks to manifest by its life and work a faithfulness to him. By designating the church as a *human community*, I underscore two points. The word human points to the church as a body of people who are both faithful and faithless, who both contribute to and disfigure life. The church is thus not a holy community in the sense of embodying purity or sacredness, or as being able to command absolute commitment or devotion. As human the church is shaped by human agency, with all its magnificent capacities and foibles.

Secondly, the church as a *human* community is affected by the congeries of drives and activities that surround it. It is neither insulated nor isolated from its environment. As a human community it is always provisional in its forms, flexible in its structures, and subject to change in its language and practices, for such are characteristics of any human enterprise that must cope with the surrounding world.

By the term *community*, I mean an organized system of interrelated elements characterized by a boundary and a functional unity. Again, the term community is subject to definitional vagueness. It may be employed to characterize a body as having certain relational components of an intimate and primary sort, as in the well-known distinction between I-Thou communities and I-You societies, the former of which is marked by personal, the latter by impersonal relations. Or the term may mean the connections assumed or proposed very broadly, as in the "community of mankind."

Again, this use is more limited. Community refers to the body of people who are related in an organized fashion to one another because of a common commitment to, and conviction about, God as known in and through Jesus Christ. Through him the nature of reality is understood and responded to. This community is not formless. It is and will be organized in a certain way. It will take on institutional forms, that is, patterns and practices of acting that have continuity across time. It will also have a boundary or boundaries. Not every one will wish to carry the appellation of Christian. It is not an ultimate judgment on persons to recognize that they are not within the community of the church. After all, it is a human community. Finally, the community is marked by a functional unity. It is united in a common function or series of functions. The church may characterize these functions programmatically as worship, witness, service, or exercise of power. Or it may denote the central function in a more normative fashion, as *shalom* or, to take two recent proposals, reconciliation, or the increase of the love of God and neighbor among men.[1] As a human community, the church will be marked by organization, boundaries, and functions.

To describe the church in such a fashion invites some further exploration. For the church as a human community has many forms of organization, diverse boundary markers as to who is or who is not a part of its fold, and it shares a functional unity only in particular cases, not in any observable universal sense. Thus, there is the First United Methodist Church of Chicago, Illinois, and the First Presbyterian Church of Tulia, Texas, two particular human communities rightly called churches. But their organizational connection is nonexistent. There is the Roman Catholic Church and the United Presbyterian Church, U.S.A., two quite diverse organizations, with differing boundary markers and disparate understandings between and within them as to their basic functional unity. Their interrelatedness is minimal or maximal, depending on the particularity of the meeting points. Or even within a denomination, which is a form of church community, there are great differences of opinion about organization, boundaries, and functional unity.

Nevertheless, I am defining the church in this fashion in order to concretize our discussion. When we use the word church we are referring to concrete human communities, those local churches and those denominational and inter-denominational groups that journalists can report as "churches." These communities are the agents of activity that are our concern. As corporate bodies they bear responsibility in the society. They have a certain kind of life. They act. Taken together their unity is a confession of faith more than an organizational realization. Their boundaries separate them from one another as well as from those who do not name Jesus Christ as Lord. But it is these bodies, including local congregations, regional associations, and national gatherings, which one must hold in mind, not some mystical body, as we investigate the church and the search for a peaceable city. Otherwise our generalizations will escape their moorings and float away from any reality base.

Further, in focusing upon the churches as particular human communities, as agents seeking a peaceable city, we are not denying or denigrating the activity of individual Christians in their various locations of power and responsibility. We assume the presence and practice of such faithfulness, although we do not consider such to be automatic or inevitable. But we are focusing on the church as a social institution with implications for the social life of man. Our concern is to consider how it may exercise its faithfulness toward *shalom*.

The symbol of *shalom* refers to the purposes of God for a universal community of creation. The *shalom* known now is a foretaste of that which is expected and sought. The seeking of a peaceable city is an exercise of movement from our current experience of its presence and absence to a more adequate manifestation and provision. Such a pilgrimage requires, among other things, hope and power, which come together in the formulation and implementation of social policies. The church is a body of people who engage in peacemaking activities, who contribute out of their experience and expectation of *shalom* to its extension and preservation among men.

The description of life as a power field, as in the preceding chapter, suggested that action is an exercise of power toward a desired end or purpose. So understood, the church's action toward *shalom* may be characterized as an exertion of power to achieve a peaceable city. All the church's activities may be evaluated by the criterion of its use or misuse of its power in the light of its purpose. Do its preaching and worship enliven and refresh the search for a peaceable city? Does its teaching define and clarify the dimensions of *shalom* in the past, present, and future, while essaying as well the current requirements for faithfulness? Does its intercourse with other institutions and groups witness to and advance the things which make for peace? Do its pronouncements expose what prevents peace while urging positive social policies?

Yet even to rehearse these questions, vital and important as they are, strikes the ear as somewhat naïve or perhaps pretentious. Their grating quality lies in the dawning consciousness of the disparity between the greatness and comprehensiveness of the purpose, *shalom*, and the power of the self-conscious agent who acts on its behalf, the church. On any grounds there appears to be little fit between the proposed purpose and the actual power. If indeed, as James Gustafson has put it, that "institutional power must be proportionate to the purposes it is supposed to achieve; or to turn it about, normative purposes that do not have proper institutional power wither away," [2] then at first glance the cause is clearly hopeless.

Indeed, a spate of recent serious and popular literature has persuasively contended that the position of the church as a powerful agent in shaping public affairs has been seriously eroded during the last several centuries. The discussion of secularization has sought to delineate two facets of this loss of power. The first is the presumption of a consciousness that is indifferent to the question of ultimate power and meaning. We have looked at that contention about the contemporary world earlier. The second is the analysis of the church as a social institution that has in historical fact lost many of its resources and powers that in an earlier time made their effect on the social order a potent one. This disestablishment of the church can be documented in its loss of large properties which made it wealthy, in its being stripped of sole or even important responsibility for the national educational tasks, and the abrogation of many of the health and welfare functions of the church by governmental and private agencies. All these were both manifestations and sources of public power for the church. It is difficult for contemporary man even to imagine a day when the archbishop of a land was the second or third most powerful personage of the realm, as was certainly the case, for example, in England during the fifteenth and early sixteenth centuries. It is even more difficult for the romantic imagination to recognize that that power rested on material bases of economic and political resources. But that is clearly the case. Shakespeare's audiences could easily identify with the offer of economic power to Henry V by the Archbishop of Canterbury:

> O, let their bodies follow, my dear liege,
> With blood and sword and fire to win your right;
> In aid whereof we of the spiritualty
> Will raise your highness such a mighty sum
> As never did the clergy at one time
> Bring in to any of your ancestors.
>
> (*King Henry* V, i. 2. 130-35)

The secularizing argument that the church has lost public power as it has lost public resources and functions is persuasive.

A second and related source of the church's loss of public power is seen to be pluralism. Pluralism points to the presence of many religious communities within a society, each vying with the others in the marketplace of commitments and convictions, each equal before the law. This splintering of the religious communities has resulted, or so it is argued, in the absence of any one having significant public power. Moreover, pluralism is not only a pattern of institutions standing equally before and under the law. It points to a type of consciousness wherein the self knows that the practical integration of his life cannot be defined by any one community or group. For the social order is too complex. Only the individual can become the arbiter of integrity within such a condition, though he may receive guidance and instruction from many sources.

We could go on. But the literature itself is familiar to most. The argument concludes that the church is a diminished giant, shorn of its previous powers in the public sphere, assigned by the emerged and emerging social order to highly limited functions. That its realm of competence is set by the social order is, indeed, the most telling argument against the church's potency. That social location has been described as ministering to the private sphere of life, to familial tensions, to wounds administered in the rough and tumble "real world." Moreover, this limited sphere of operation has not only been assigned by the social order. It has too often been embraced by the churches. They have been deprived of that which defined their nature and function—the ability to contribute toward the peaceable city.

While this type of analysis of the church has been tempered somewhat by the active engagement of the churches in the human struggles for human rights and for more humane conditions on a worldwide basis, the experience of the churches and of churchmen has in recent decades ratified the previous analysis. The awareness of the rift between their aspirations for *shalom* and their own limitations has been a cultural experience. Perhaps the emergence of one-world has provided the contemporary Western churches with a culture shock greater than any analysis of their social location ever could. For the vital presence of one world has meant the expansion of consciousness to recognize that the Christian faith is a minority faith in a world of many faiths and convictions.

Further, the displacement of the West as the assumed center and highest manifestation of civilization has been accomplished by an enlarging horizon of cultures, each with its own ingredients of value. For centuries the Christian churches had assumed that they had a crucial role to play in the formation of the Western world, and that Western civilization would be a carrier of genuinely superior humanizing powers throughout the world. Now, however, both the West and the churches of the West have been stripped of their innocence. There is no longer any basis for an assumed superiority on the part of the West. The reason for this loss is not only the recognition of the power and worth of other cultures. It is as well a recognition of the West's own implication in evil.

Dietrich Bonhoeffer noted this loss of the West as an assumed carrier of humanizing powers, identifying the critical event as the presence of total war. He wrote:

It is only when Christian faith is lost that man must himself make use of all means, even criminal ones, in order to secure by force the victory of his cause. And thus, in the place of a chivalrous war between Christian peoples, directed towards the achievement of unity in accordance with God's judgment in history, there comes total war, war of destruction, in which everything, even crime, is justified if it serves to further his own cause, and in which the enemy, whether he be armed or defenceless, is treated as a criminal. Only with the advent of total war is there a threat to the unity of the west. . . .

By the loss of the unity which it possessed through the form of Jesus Christ, the western world is brought to the brink of the void. The forces unleashed exhaust their fury in mutual destruction. Everything established is threatened with annihilation. This is not a crisis among other crises. It is a decisive struggle of the last days. . . . The void engulfs life, history, family, nation, language, faith. The list can be prolonged indefinitely, for the void spares nothing.[3]

The philosopher Henry David Aiken has noted the same alteration in the consciousness of the West. He writes:

The Spanish Civil War marks the beginning of a great sea change in the attitudes of Western men toward their whole civilization.

. . . For this was the moment at which there set in a vague but sickening sense of general cultural disorder, of imponderable ideological conflicts and moral duplicities, of pervasive institutional incompetence and corruption. Nor was the malaise limited merely to "the others"; that is, to the Fascists, Nazis, Communists, and other "totalitarian" monsters unlike ourselves. On the contrary, it also afflicted the liberal democracies, the Christian churches, the universities: in short, all the presumptive traditional carriers of political and social progress, moral regeneration, and intellectual enlightenment. With the onset of the Second World War, there was momentarily a superficial clearing of the moral air. . . . Soon, however, the whole world found itself involved in a new round of paradoxes whose very terms no one seemed able to comprehend. How, for example, does one cope with total war save by responding in kind? [4]

So conceived, the impotence of the Christian church, identified as it has been with the development of Western civilization, is more severe than has been suggested by social analyses of the place of the church in the West. The last source of presumptive power, the West itself, has been undermined by its own inhumane practices of total war, not to mention racism and economic exploitation of colonial peoples. It is the combination of one-world with its richness and variety of cultures with the exposure of the abyss of evil within the West that has caused a crisis of confidence about the adequacy of the power available to the church to move toward *shalom*. By adequacy, I mean not only the magnitude of power available but its appropriateness for the purpose.

This array of charges about the inadequacy of the power of the churches adds to the sense of dichotomy between the purpose of *shalom* and the proportionate power available to the churches. Does that dichotomy mean, then, that the

SHALOM: THE SEARCH FOR A PEACEABLE CITY

normative purpose is doomed to wither away, flawed not by its beauty but condemned by its environment?

To answer yes to such an inquiry would be to confuse the referent of the theological symbol of *shalom* with a human enterprise. *Shalom* as an eschatological symbol refers to God's intentions for his creation. God is he who is the sacred power, who is sufficient for what he purposes. To affirm *shalom* is not to affirm the power of the church or churches. Nor is it to identify the requisite power for *shalom* with any historical epoch, whether Western civilization or the technological age. The affirmation of *shalom* is an affirmation of God's power that is effecting his purpose now and will bring his creation to fruition. His power, Christians affirm, is proportionate to his purpose. In the movement toward a peaceable city God uses many agents. In Isaiah it is Cyrus the Assyrian who is his servant as certainly as is Israel (Isa. 41:2 ff.). Yahweh stirs up the Medes to overthrow the Babylonians (Isa. 13:17 ff.). In the New Testament, Jesus counts as his friends those who do his Father's will, not those necessarily who call him Lord (Matt. 7: 21 ff.). Even Pilate's power derives from God (John 19:11). What the churches are to do is to respond to that sacred power who is working throughout his creation, wherever they may discern his intentions being advanced.

The church then witnesses, even as it responds, to God's activity. The church does not foster the illusory hope among its own constituents, nor among others, that it will of its own power effect *shalom*. But it confesses that God is working toward *shalom* and seeks gratefully to respond to his leading. The church hopes in God.

But to hope in God is to hope in, with, and for the neighbor. The church's response to God will take many forms as it contributes to the well-being and the well-doing

192

of the peaceable city. These forms will inevitably be shaped by the social location of the church. But they need not be determined by the social order's designation of some limited province. Even as the symbol of *shalom* comprehends the full range of life, so the church seeks a peaceable city that will contribute to the humane life of each person and for all the citizens. We have argued already that one important contribution of the church for itself and others is the affirmation of an eschatological symbol that will accord with the society's genuine needs.[5] We will now look briefly at three programmatic ways by which the church that finds itself a member of Western civilization may contribute to the social life of the emerging worldwide city of man. These are (1) the nurture of subsystems; (2) theological contextualizing of issues; and (3) coalitional involvement. In selecting these three, I am not excluding others, only focusing on important opportunities for the church.

In the discussion of the church as a social institution relegated to providing services for the essentially private and familial life of man, there has been both an implicit and explicit negative evaluation of that responsibility. One source of such criticism has been that such an emphasis served to distract the church and its constituents from the broader vistas of God's call and claim. The effect of the church's social location in relation to the family, with the consequent shaping of a program that such a location required, meant that inevitably the broader social issues were accorded scant attention or, even more seriously, the social order was blessed as "the best of all possible worlds." The criticism was that the transcendent claim of God was domesticated to patching up quarrels, baby-sitting services, the reassurance of value and worth, and a source of pleasant diversions. The sharp spearpoint of this attack was also directed against the main-

193

line white Protestant churches' withdrawal from the urban context of racial minorities and poverty. The argument was, in shorthand, that the church, itself a subsystem of a macrosystem, was relating only to one other subsystem, the family, and excluding from its purview the broader and more consequential issues of the nature of the whole system and/or of the more significant political and economic subsystems.

Few today would deny that such analyses and criticisms of the churches were appropriate. Indeed the churches' own highly valued professional skills have been those that could deal with the management of individual problems rather than with conflict management within and between groups and institutions, whether in or outside the church.[6] Personal counseling, for example, has been isolated as a desirable and required art for pastors, a skill in accord with the therapeutic needs of parishioners. No one or few desired to negate the importance of pastoral counseling. It was the imbalance of emphasis on such pastoral, as contrasted with prophetic, functions which was the object of attack.

Yet the social location of the churches in relation to the familial subsystem might well be interpreted not only as a liability. It might rather be viewed as an asset. For it is by no means proved that the family is an impotent institution in shaping the future. Indeed, the argument could just as cogently be made that the family remains a crucial social matrix in providing either an enabling or disabling context for the growth and development of persons. The family certainly affects basic moods and motivations. It mediates attitudes and dispositions and values to and among adults and children. It is a social nexus for verbalizing and acting out hopes and expectations, frustrations and failures. It engenders persisting moods and motivations.

That the family is often blamed today for its negative

194

effects upon its members testifies to, rather than denies, its potency as a social institution. For the family not only is itself a matrix for the formation of selfhood but also influences the particular social matrices into which its minority members may be fed. For example, in the contemporary period the family shares with the adolescent peer group in influencing the life of teen-agers. But the family still has a significant degree of control over the peer group with which its children associate. It exercises such influence by its choice of housing and by its selection of schools.

Also, there is no clear and convincing evidence that the so-called private and familial sphere has no influence on the more public spheres. The evidence would seem rather to indicate that there is not so much a separation between the private and the public lives of selves as there is a coherence. The values and commitments exercised in the political sphere have a correspondence with the values and commitments realized in the social life of the family. The economic aspirations of the self in the economic world are mirrored in the material expectations and styles of the family. Such a coherence may indeed be a problem, for the quality of the correspondence may be one that contributes toward the dehumanizing of life in both the public and private spheres. But the assumption of a radical split between such spheres is highly debatable and thus far unproved.

Further, there has been an assumption that, if there is a connection between the public and private spheres, the flow of influence is heavily asymmetrical, a one-way stream from the former to the latter, so that any input into the ordering of the public realm from the arenas of church and family is comparable to the swim of the female salmon from the ocean up the river to her birthplace. The obstacles are fierce, and any who did make it would perish if they reached their goal!

But if the family remains a potent social institution for affecting life, as I am persuaded it is, then the church's location socially may be interpreted as providing unique access to persons. The church-family connection may be visualized as a potentially positive one that recognizes that in a pluralistic society, marked by many communities of loyalty, the church as one such center must vie with others in urging and altering values and commitments. But its social access to the family provides it with an entryway into one subsystem affecting the public order denied to others. How it chooses to use that access and entryway, whether to affirm what is and only to patch up quarrels, or to provide for the interpretation of life as one of seeking *shalom*, is another question. But the opportunity for influence is present.

For the familial subsystem is never an isolated subsystem. By definition it is a part of the whole social fabric. Thus any issue confronting the total system impinges upon families. For example, the Vietnam War became an issue for the family directly, as sons and daughters, grandchildren and nephews and nieces faced the immediate issue of their stance toward this undeclared war. When a son is facing the draft, the issue of a war or of war in general becomes no longer merely a family issue. It is a question of the shape of the public order. At such a time the concrete question of the draft and of war-making can be addressed by the church, indeed must be so addressed if it is to minister to the family. Such attention will not be free from strife and contention, as has been documented recently in the United States as churches developed programs of draft-counseling. But the broad societal policy issue can be and must be faced by families at such a time. The church's access to the family provides it with an opportunity for exploring what makes for peace in the contemporary world.

One could give other examples. The provision by a national church body of funds for the legal defense of a black militant impinges upon the families of local white, middle-class churches. The medium is the sense of proprietorship and financial commitments to the ecclesiastical system owned by local church members. Such an incident may be an occasion for considering the nature of the legal system in the society and of the role of the church in public advocacy. Or it may be the occasion for repudiating any responsibility for broad human issues by the church. But the broader systemic issue is raised. Or the withholding of church-owned shares in polluting companies raises for individuals and families the question of how their economic power shall be stewarded. The point is that all public issues become or can become personal and familial issues. The opportunity for the church in its relation with the family and through the family to the broader social policy questions is a fertile one.

In contributing to the peaceable city the church's relation to the familial subsystem can be highly significant. It can be that in the long-range nurturing of the members of the family, in their search for meaning and direction.[7] It can be that as well as it operates on the assumption of the interconnection of the public and the private spheres of life. To be a servant of *shalom* and to serve the familial units, the church in its own variety of systems, from local to international, must be itself engaged in attempting to shape the larger systems through actions and pronouncements. Not to do so is to withhold from the families of the church what they genuinely require—an enacted knowledge that it is the totality of life which affects them and which they as peacemakers are called upon to affect. Particular families may reject such a recognition, but in doing so they diminish and distort their own lives. Such families destroy their peace. For peace for the family and its members cannot be obtained apart from peace for the social order. For the church to pronounce a blessing of "Peace" upon families without seeking peace throughout the systems of life is to cry, "Peace, peace, when there is no peace."

A second way by which the church contributes to the formulation and implementation of social policies that make for peace is by a theological contextualizing of issues. I have hinted at the importance of that function in the illustration above about war as a social issue and about how it impinges upon the individual and the familial social unit. Thus, this function is not separate from our previous consideration, though its ramifications go beyond those of speaking only to familial constituents. Theological contextualization—an unfortunately cumbersome phrase—attempts to address the broader public issues and therefore the broader public.

Theological contextualization is a phrase designed to indicate the task of interpreting human events, aspirations, and movements in the light of basic theological symbols. The theological symbol, I have contended, provides an illumining perspective on present and emerging activities and expectations. It provides an ultimate context in which they can be analyzed, clarified, and evaluated. The goal of such analysis, clarification, and evaluation is a reformulation of understanding and activity by agents, individual and corporate, so that the response to God in and through his creation may be more appropriate to his intentions and activity.

The call for theological contextualizing is similar in intention to Dietrich Bonhoeffer's call for a "religionless interpretation of the gospel." The focus is upon human activities, movements, and expectations, seeking to locate them not in their relation to any particular religious community but to the intentions of God for all his creation. There is no avoidance of the penultimate. There is the attempt to contextualize the penultimate in terms of God's intentions for human well-being and well-doing.

Theological contextualizing is as well an echo of H. Richard Niebuhr's description of *interpretation* as one movement within the life of responsibility before God and man. Niebuhr wrote, "All actions that go on within the sphere of our bodies, from heartbeats to knee jerks, are doubtless also reactions, but they do not fall within the domain of self-actions if they are not accompanied and infused . . . with interpretation . . . . We interpret the things that force themselves upon us as parts of wholes, as related and as symbolic of larger meanings. And these large patterns of interpretation we employ seem to determine—though in no mechanical way—our response to action upon us." [8] Niebuhr illustrates this with reference to Jesus. "If we try to summarize the ethos of Jesus in a formula we may do so by saying that he interprets all actions upon him as signs of the divine action of creation, government and salvation and so responds to them as to respond to divine action." [9] Thus, a crucial function for the church is to interpret human life in the context of God's action. It has no more significant task, for it is in such interpretation that the concrete struggle between commitment to God and commitment to idols is exposed. It is in fulfilling this function that the church addresses the conscious and unconscious frames of reference that inform perception and action.

The church fulfills the function of theological contextualizing through many media. Preaching, teaching, study, pronouncements, actions—all these are vehicles for the task.

We can illustrate briefly how theological contextualizing treats human issues by looking at the human yearning for a peaceful world with which we began our whole investigation.

The cry for peace which rises from a world weary of war, rumors of war, and preparations for the next war reflects a generation that hardly knows how to think of peace without thinking of war. As a result, the term peace has become for most the mirror image of the term war. Peace has come to mean absence of war. Thus the cry for peace becomes a cry to "Stop the War," whatever the particular war in process might then be.

Further, thinking about what makes for peace has often been switched in the Christian community onto the siding of thinking about war. Certainly since the Constantinian settlement, when the church began to influence political thought and activity directly, a great deal of attention has been given to a consideration of whether or not and/or under what conditions the use of armed force might be justified for the followers of the Prince of Peace. The intention in all such discussion was manifestly that of providing for a humane order of existence in the midst of a sinful world. To do so required the imposition of armed sanctions, of force, against those who would attack the innocent, plunder human rights and property, and forcefully assert their own interests. Thus, there evolved the just war doctrine, setting forth conditions that justified a nation's engagement in war and restraints upon the means to be employed.

Alongside those who recognized and advocated the tragic and mournful necessity of war were always those Christian groups and individuals whose loyalty to God impelled them to reject taking up arms against their neighbors, no matter what the external conditions. The "peace churches," for so the groups espousing a complete disavowal of armed force came to be called, reflected by their appellation that peace meant primarily abstaining from war. That was certainly not the intention of such groups, but the necessity to defend themselves against charges of disloyalty to the nation arose in times of war and imposed upon them the necessity to define themselves in the public mind over against the reality of war.[10]

Both these perspectives concerning the issue of the legitimate use of force by Christians and others have been and remain important still today as the church and others seek to think and to act in a world that harbors fearful weaponry and governments that could and would engage in war. But what is sorely lacking and required is a new context for thinking about and acting toward peace. Such is necessary if nations are not to be deluded into thinking that ending hostilities is all that is required for peace. It is needed lest peoples weary of war think they have contributed all that is necessary when they have brought a war to its conclusion, whether that be victory, defeat, or some negotiated settlement. Too often the exhaustion with war has led a weary people at the close of the fighting to be concerned only for a return to life as usual, to demobilization, and to getting on with private concerns. As that occurs, the preparation and energies expended for "peace" begin to channel themselves into defense budgets that will "preserve the peace." And again peace becomes defined by war.

The theological symbol of *shalom* provides a different context for the human yearning for peace. It encompasses the search for ways to end both particular wars and war in general. While encouraging activity toward those ends, it is not thereby exhausted of content. It defines peace as a form of relatedness among all persons where there is health, security, and wholeness for all. Peace is understood as a positive involvement of all persons with their neighbors in the increase of well-being and well-doing. Peacemaking is not an intermittent task, provoked by the outbreak of armed conflict. It is an ongoing responsibility, requiring diligent activity toward the reconstituting of human life on all levels, from the individual through the institutional, and in all spheres, from the local through the international arenas of existence. The search for a peaceable city is a more comprehensive goal and task than ending the war.

Shalom as a comprehensive symbol therefore stands in contradiction to the present experience of men in a variety of areas, not just in the presence of armed conflict. It contradicts all those human practices and institutions that disfigure life. All those contradictions become directional pointers for the construction of new ways of human interactions and organizations that will more nearly approximate the peace which God intends.

Thus, within a nation such as the United States, the task of peacemaking requires the rooting out of racism within institutions, the empowering of persons through more adequate and humane educational systems, the provision of economic resources for all, the delivery of health care for those requiring it, the opening up of political systems to provide for more accountability, and the nurturing of persons through new patterns of caring. The search for a peaceable city directs attention to human need wherever it may be found and whatever its form, whether it be a result of conscious or unconscious activity, the consequence of an omission of concern or of a commission of exploitation.

Shalom calls for the enactment of social policies that will be agents of hope and power.

In all this, *shalom* as a theological symbol recontextualizes the yearning for peace. It defines peace not only as the absence of war, but as a positive task that involves a wide range of engagement with the needs of men. The specificity of what makes for peace in any particular situation or time requires detailed analysis and strategies for action, of course. But peacemaking in all its richness and complexity becomes an ongoing and initiatory activity, not just a reaction to an overt defect in the relationship between nations.

But *shalom* applies not only within national boundaries. *Shalom* as a universal symbol seeks to foster univeral responsibility, to advance a comprehensive community of mankind. As a comprehensive symbol its intention is to effect new forms of peacemaking which transcend limited boundaries, whether of churches or nations.

Clearly the symbol of *shalom* accords well with the recent emergence of a worldwide society in which the material connectedness of the whole world is evidenced by the jet plane, the H-bomb, and television. It is this worldwide context for life which requires such a comprehensive and universal symbol. It is this context that requires a new consciousness for man, which can be translated into new responses to the surrounding environment. *Shalom* seeks to be a midwife to such a new consciousness.

Yet it is also clear that for many their consciousness and therefore their positive activities remain shaped by previous configurations of relationships among men. For such persons and groups the only genuine reality of consciousness requiring positive care and attention may be the nation-state or perhaps Western civilization. The result is an active indifference or hostility to a consideration of an international or universal context for responsibility. Yet the peaceable city, anticipated by the prophets, expected by Jesus, and longed for by the church, is a worldwide city in which justice and righteousness prevail among the whole community of creation. An obvious contradiction is present between the hope of *shalom* and the present limited range of consciousness and responsibility infecting large numbers of persons.

Perhaps the clearest contradiction on a worldwide scale between the expected and sought *shalom* and the current experience of life is that between the rich and the poor nations of the world. The figures that evidence such a disparity have been widely reported, even if their meaning has not been absorbed. I shall cite only one. One fourth of the world's population now consumes eighty percent of the world's goods. Conversely, three fourths of the world's population have only twenty percent of the world's goods. And the rich one fourth of the population is concentrated primarily in the developed countries of the West, with the addition of the U.S.S.R. But such cold figures hide the human realities of affluence versus poverty, obesity versus malnutrition, comfortable shelters versus exposure, long-life expectation versus early death, which form the contours of radically different types of existence.

The sources of this dichotomy between rich and poor are multiple. One lies in the ironies of Western political and economic imperialism. For both the prospect and the problem of a worldwide city were mediated through that collection of movements. Peter Worsley has noted this paradox. "Europe had accomplished a transformation which created the world as a social system. It was a world-order founded on conquest and maintained by force . . . . At the one pole stood industrialized Europe; at the other, the disinherited.

Paradoxically the world had been divided in the process of its unification, divided into spheres of influence, and divided into rich and poor." [11]

The initial movement of the poor sectors of the world, coming to a head immediately after World War II, was for political independence. Thus, the targets for attack were the colonizing nations, Great Britain and France being the most vivid examples. During the struggle for political independence, nations such as the United States, which had only minimal direct political control over other peoples, were fairly immune from charges of exploitation. But the struggle for economic independence which was and is layered onto the struggle for political autonomy implicated all the modern industrialized countries, those on both sides of the Iron Curtain. The need and drive for economic development soon replaced the call for decolonization by the poor nations of the world. The plight of their peoples was desperate and, with mounting population pressures and rising expectation, would show no natural slackening.

Further, the economic structures established between the rich and poor nations in earlier days—the colonies provided raw materials and a market for industrialized, "advanced" nations—meant a continued dependence upon the rich nations, which led to the rich getting richer and the poor staying poor or getting poorer. It was this situation that led to the commitment by many nations to the Development Decade, inaugurated under United Nations' auspices in 1961. That has now been replaced by the Second Development Decade, to span the seventies. The purpose of both has been and is the recognition by the rich nations of their obligations to the peoples of the poor nations, and their consequent adoption of trade and aid programs that will alleviate and overcome eventually the glaring imbalance between rich and poor. The results thus far have been mixed, with indeed the United States' contribution to development efforts falling in terms of the ratio of its Gross National Product, the percentage falling between 1960 and 1970 from 0.79% to 0.61%.

This cursory glance at the worldwide situation is designed only to signal that the human search for a peaceable city requires a new consciousness of the world as one and a resultant commitment to discern and implement ways that the well-being and well-doing of all, the rich and the poor, may be advanced. Such a task awaits the recognition within the rich countries of the issue and their place in meeting it, and on the construction of highly technical international trade and aid programs that will concretize that consciousness. It awaits both a new social consciousness and new social policies. *Shalom* as a theological symbol seeks to mediate both to the church and to the world.

The theological contextualizing of peace therefore embraces the search for material well-being, health, and security for all the peoples of the world. Pope Paul VI dramatized this type of theological contextualizing in 1967 in his encyclical letter *Populorum Progressio*. After surveying the range of human needs present on a worldwide scale, Paul concluded by imploring Christians of all persuasions to join all men of goodwill in a commitment to the material and political development of persons and nations. He wrote, "For if the new name for peace is development, who would not wish to labor for it with all his powers?" [12]

"Development is the new name for peace!" That slogan still searches for an effective program. The churches in their interpretation of the things that make for peace can contribute to the emergence of a consciousness and a commitment toward the peaceable city that will eventuate in the development of the rich and the poor toward a social order measured by the quality of the relatedness among peoples rather than the quantitative disparity between rich and poor. Such a vision of, and activity toward, that universal city might indeed do as much for the rich as for the poor, offering them a new sense of purpose and meaning to replace the failed minimal gods of private economic success and status. For the enlarging of the self depends upon the enlarging of his world of commitment and responsibility. The symbol of *shalom* carries the promise of a more fulfilled humanity for all, as all engage in the search for a worldwide peaceable city.

In the paragraphs above I have attempted to illustrate how the theological symbol of *shalom* provides a new context for the human yearning for peace. I have suggested that *shalom* engages the human cries for peace, whatever their source and object. Such longings may express a desire only for the ending of hostilities between two nations, or for the need for national tranquillity. They may rise up out of fear of destruction and death. Whatever their meaning, *shalom* provides a theological context that seeks to transform these yearnings. It does so by recognizing their genuineness, but relocating them within a context that more authentically reflects what will contribute to human well-being and welldoing, a context of universal responsibility.

Theological contextualizing of human issues, whatever they may be, judges the limited location and understanding of those issues and enriches and expands their dimensions. Its goal is a new consciousness and different forms of activity. It is an ongoing process for the church. "A sustained interpretation and critique of society is required from the perspective of the community that acknowledges that there is no authority except from God." [13]

207

Theological contextualizing must be linked with activity by the churches, if it is to be authentic. Preaching, teaching, and inquiry by the church into human issues and their proper context are joined with action appropriate to the understanding. The two go together, action and reflection, feeding each other.

A third way by which the church contributes toward the peaceable city is in its activity on behalf of social policies and programs. One form of such activity may be characterized as coalitional. Such a style is appropriate to a pluralistic world where there are many patterns of belief, many communities of concern, and diversity within and between religious communities. Within such a diverse setting there is no possible or necessary agreement about ultimate concerns. Indeed, there is not even any theological consensus that could unite all the churches. What is present is the ability of groups to come together from time to time on relative social programs and policies to be supported. The point of meeting when that occurs is not a common creed or ultimate commitment. It is a recognition of a common human problem and/or prospect that elicits active support.

A coalition is composed of persons and groups from a variety of perspectives, who converge together to support a social policy or program of mutual concern and interest. Churches committed to *shalom* concretize programmatically what such a commitment means for the social order as they isolate issues to be confronted and policies to be advanced. In doing so they find that they are usually not alone in their concern. They may be joined by, or may themselves join, other voluntary associations, community organizations, interest groups, political movements, or religious communities. In doing so the churches may react to stimuli that come from outside their boundaries, coming as a late partner to the struggle. Or they may initiate activity designed to alter the current conditions of life. Churches so acting must organize or evoke support from others if they are to be effective in their use of social power. In the pluralistic world, churches themselves seldom bear social power proportionate to their purposes. For example, churches lack the power to bend the direction of American foreign policy in such a way that it is oriented toward providing increasing resources for the poor nations of the world. But they can coalesce with other groups and interests in a common endeavor toward that social policy. Indeed, the coalition may include those who do not number themselves as members. It may be interpreted as broadly as to comprehend the demands exerted on the United States government by third-world authorities and groups. It is the issue which defines the coalitional community, not the acknowledged membership.

In a coalition there are diverse interests at stake. The church's stated interest is peacemaking, the search for a peaceable city. But it recognizes the power of self-interest among its partners and within itself. It does not identify such self-interest as invariably evil but acknowledges that the interest of *shalom* does unite from time to time with the self-interest of groups. Thus, in the early days of the civil rights movement it was clearly to the self-interest of the blacks to attain equal access to public accommodations. But such interest was judged as not divergent from the search for a peaceable city. On other occasions there is no such convergence.

We must be clear that coalition means a temporary union for a common purpose. It does not mean merger. A coalition depends on, and is strengthened by, each group's maintaining a sense of its own identity and integrity. The church which acts coalitionally must be aware of its own reasons for acting and be willing to particularize those if called upon to do so. It is the particularity of the various members of the coalition which supplements and complements the others that come together, both in terms of goal and in terms of strategy.

Finally, coalition creates new and promising communities that are themselves foretastes of the eschatological *shalom*. The experience of the church in the recent struggles for social policies related to civil rights, peace, economic development, environment, and social reform has often been a heightened sense of fellowship for the participants with their fellowmen. Many persons so engaged have testified that they found in such activities a genuine and authentic sense of being at peace with themselves and with their neighbors, both those whom they called colleagues and those whom they opposed. Such an experience was more profound than the conflict which also marked their participation in such movements. They knew peace as an interaction with their neighbors embracing faith, hope, love, forgiveness, and power.

But a coalition is always temporary, provisional, a fragmentary part of life. By definition coalitions dissolve as issues change, gains are made, and new concerns arise. Thus these meaningful experiences also become memories, and perhaps foretastes of new communities yet to be. But when they are experienced and recalled, they shine forth for Christians and the church as at least partial fulfillments of the promise of *shalom*. They become the signs and seals of the eschatological peace that is broader than beliefs and more inclusive than sects, but which is genuinely humanizing, where all come from East and West, North and South, and sit down together in peace at the table of the Lord. They were genuine occasions for celebration and rejoicing. Thus the experience of coalition can even serve to revivify the separate communities called churches. For they provide a fresh sense of the present power of God to provide a context for life that is enabling and fulfilling. They become concrete signs of hope in God and in, for, and with the neighbor.

For some, of course, participation in one such coalition becomes the bright event of life, unrepeatable, unsurpassable. Those persons become fixated on that occasion. Everything else now seems desert-like, unable to carry the wonder of that time. If and when such fixation occurs, the coalitional activity was the termination of the self's or the church's peacemaking. It ceases to be a sign of the presence of God throughout his creation, bringing together people over and over again to engage in the labor toward *shalom*. It becomes itself an occasion draining the self and/or the church of the potency of responding to the continuing rule of God.

But in a dynamic and pluralistic world, churches as well as individuals must move from coalition to coalition. The constant emergence of new issues and concerns guarantees that a realignment of coalitions is inevitable, as new social policies are required to provide for the peaceable city.

We have looked briefly at three modes of activity holding promise for the churches as peacemakers. There are numerous others that could be reported and that remain to be discovered. The search for a peaceable city requires versatility and imagination, creativity and persistence, reflection and action, and all poured into styles of activity that are pertinent to the concrete needs of men and reflective of the hope for *shalom*. There is no one way into the peaceable city. There are many approaches to its environs and many strategies for its achievement.

But that the peaceable city is coming is the conviction of Christians. That its coming is urgent is the cry of all men. That he will bring it to completion is the promise of God. That he invites our participation in its coming is announced in this fashion: "Blessed are the peacemakers, for they shall be called sons of God" (Matt. 5:9).

Notes

Introduction

1. Within Protestant ethical thought, Joseph Fletcher's *Situation Ethics* (Philadelphia: The Westminster Press, 1966) and Paul Ramsey's *Deeds and Rules in Christian Ethics* (New York: Charles Scribner's Son's, 1967) are representative of the poles between which the argument has moved. Both are primarily essays concerned with the *necessary* force of the diverse elements of Christian ethical reflection. Fletcher's study champions the significance of individual decision making finally unencumbered by principles and rules, though informed by maxims. Ramsey's work presses for the elaboration of principles and rules that are entailed by the *agape* of God and that require the assent of Christian decision makers. Other ethicists have participated in this discussion. Some have clarified the broader methodological framework in which the discussion between situation and rules emphases should be set. James M. Gustafson's article, "Rules vs. Deeds: A Misplaced Debate," *The Harvard Theological Review*, April, 1965, is one example. Still others, such as Gibson Winter in his *Elements of a Social Ethic* (New York: The Macmillan Co., 1966), James Sellers in his *Theological Ethics* (New York: The Macmillan Co., 1966), and James M. Gustafson in *Christ and the Moral Life* (New York: Harper & Row, 1968), have proposed alternative frames of reference. But the dominant methodological debate has focused upon the bearing of rules and situations upon Christian decision making.

2. The tenacity of *agape* as the primary ethical norm in both academic and ecclesiastical circles is remarkable. While there are diverse interpretations of the content of love, love dominates the scene. James M. Gustafson has pointed out, for example, how such disparate ways of doing ethics as those embraced by Paul Ramsey and Joseph Fletcher still unite on *agape* as the central criterion. Cf. James M. Gustafson, "How Does Love Reign?" *The Christian Century*, May 18, 1966.

3. Quoted by John W. Aldridge, "The Enormous Spider Web of Warren's World," *Saturday Review*, October 9, 1971, p. 36.

Chapter I. The Search for a Peaceable City.

1. St. Augustine, *The City of God*, Book XIX, Ch. 11. *The Fathers of the Church*, V. 24, tr. by Gerald G. Walsh, S.J., and Daniel J. Honan (Washington: Catholic University of America Press, 1954), pp. 211, 212.
2. R. A. Markus, *Saeculum. History and Society in the Theology of St. Augustine* (Cambridge: The University Press, 1970), p. 68. See also John Burnaby, *Amor Dei* (London: Hodder & Stoughton, 1938), for a discussion of the loves that animate the self.
3. St. Augustine, *The City of God*, Book XIX, Ch. XVII, ed. by R. V. G. Tasker (London: J. M. Dent & Sons, 1945), p. 255.
4. *Ibid.*, Ch. XXVII, p. 266.
5. John H. S. Burleigh, *The City of God* (London: James Nisbet & Co., 1949), p. v.
6. John XXIII, *Pacem in Terris* (London: Ridge Press, 1964), p. 7.
7. *Ibid.*, p. 155.
8. "Pastoral Constitution on the Church in the Modern World," *Documents of Vatican II*, ed. by Walter M. Abbott, S.J. (New York: Association Press, 1966), p. 297.
9. See the perceptive article by Peter L. Berger, "Between Tyranny and Chaos," *The Christian Century*, October 30, 1968, pp. 1365-70.
10. David L. Edwards, *Religion and Change* (London: Hodder & Stoughton, 1969), p. 16.
11. Dietrich Bonhoeffer, *Letters and Papers from Prison*, ed. by Eberhard Bethge, trans. by R. Fuller (New York: The Macmillan Co., 1954), pp. 106, 107.
12. Harvey Cox, *The Secular City* (New York: The Macmillan Co., 1965), p. 60.
13. *Ibid.*, p. 1.
14. *Ibid.*
15. *Ibid.*, cf. the Introduction and Chapter I.
16. *Ibid.*, p. 60.
17. *Ibid.*
18. *Ibid.*, pp. 60, 61.
19. Cox in a later work, *The Feast of Fools* (Cambridge: Harvard University Press, 1969), has suggested that life's richness cannot be encompassed by a secular framework.
20. Robert O. Johann, *Building the Human* (New York: Herder and Herder, 1968), pp. 21, 22.
21. *Ibid.*, p. 17.
22. *Ibid.*
23. Dietrich Bonhoeffer, *Ethics*, ed. by Eberhard Bethge, trans. by Neville Horton Smith (New York: The Macmillan Co., 1955), p. 86.
24. *Ibid.*, p. 88.
25. *Ibid.*

26. *Ibid.*, p. 91.
27. *Ibid.*, pp. 99, 100.
28. Cox, *The Secular City*, p. 263.
29. Two important books come to mind that deal with the inevitability and necessity of an institutional and organizational location for the church's witness. One is James M. Gustafson's *Treasure in Earthen Vessels* (New York: Harper & Row, 1961). Another is Robert C. Worley's *Change in the Church: A Source of Hope* (Philadelphia: The Westminster Press, 1971). Cf. also Louis Dupré, "Religion in a Secular World," *Christianity and Crisis*, April 15, 1968, pp. 73-77.
30. Cited by Charles H. Long in his essay, "Silence and Signification: A Note on Religion and Modernity," in *Myths and Symbols*, ed. by Joseph M. Kitagawa and Charles H. Long (Chicago: University of Chicago Press, 1969), p. 144.

Chapter II. Symbols and Social Life.

1. H. Richard Niebuhr, "Reformation: Continuing Imperative," *The Christian Century*, March 2, 1960, p. 251.
2. Harvey Cox, *The Feast of Fools*, pp. 84-87.
3. Mary Douglas, *Natural Symbols* (London: Barrie & Rockliff, 1970), p. 1.
4. *Ibid.*, p. 3.
5. Suzanne Langer, *Philosophy in a New Key* (New York: New American Library, 1948), p. 237.
6. Mircea Eliade, *Images and Symbols* (London: Harvill Press, 1961), p. 19.
7. There are of course other than verbal symbols.
8. James Luther Adams, "The Pragmatic Theory of Meaning." Unpublished essay.
9. Paul Tillich, *Systematic Theology* (Chicago: University of Chicago Press, 1951), V. I, 239.
10. *Ibid.*, p. 240. See also Paul Tillich, *Dynamics of Faith* (New York: Harper & Brothers, 1958), pp. 41 ff.
11. Hugh Dalziel Duncan, *Language and Literature in Society* (Chicago: University of Chicago Press, 1953), p. vii. Cf. the discussion on naming God in Harvey Cox, *The Secular City*, pp. 172, 173.
12. Robert N. Bellah, *Religion and Progress in Modern Asia* (Glencoe: The Free Press, 1965), pp. 172, 173.
13. Cf. the discussion by Albert Dondeyne in his *Faith and the World* (Pittsburgh: Duquesne University Press, 1963).
14. Clifford Geertz, "Religion as a Cultural System," *Anthropological Approaches to the Study of Religion*, ed. by Michael Banton (New York: Frederick A. Praeger, 1966), p. 4.

15. Peter L. Berger and Thomas Luckmann, *The Social Construction of Reality* (Garden City, N. Y.: Doubleday & Co., 1967) p. 21.
16. *Ibid.*, p. 22.
17. Cf. Thomas S. Kuhn, *The Structure of Scientific Revolutions* (Chicago: University of Chicago Press, 1962), for a discussion of this phenomenon in the realm of scientific exploration.
18. Berger and Luckmann, *The Social Construction of Reality*, p. 40.
19. *Ibid.* Italics mine.
20. Robert N. Bellah, *Beyond Belief* (New York: Harper & Row, 1970), p. 261.
21. *Ibid.*, p. 261.
22. Geertz, "Religion as a Cultural System," p. 6.
23. Cf. Max Weber, *The Protestant Ethic and the Spirit of Capitalism* (New York: Charles Scribner's Sons, 1956), for one discussion of how a religious orientation powerfully influenced proximate economic activity.
24. Geertz, "Religion as a Cultural System," p. 10.
25. *Ibid.*, pp. 11, 12.
26. *Ibid.*, p. 41.
27. Lewis Mumford, *The Condition of Man*, Portuguese edition, p. 358, as cited by Rubem A. Alves, "Theology and the Condition of Man," *In Search of a Theology of Development* (Geneva: The Committee on Society, Development and Peace, n.d.), p. 77.
28. H. Richard Niebuhr, *The Responsible Self* (New York: Harper & Row, 1963), pp. 151-54.
29. David Little, *Religion, Order, and Law* (New York: Harper & Row, 1969), p. 23.
30. Herbert W. Richardson, *Toward an American Theology* (New York: Harper & Row, 1969), p. 24.
31. I am not maintaining that peace should be the exclusive or even enduring symbol. But it may be one within the Christian symbol system. H. Richard Niebuhr clarifies the multiple symbols the Christian faith employs at any one time in its history when he writes: "Now it is doubtless true that we cannot interpret the Christian life without reference to the Christ-symbol. There would be no meaning in calling it Christian life . . . if we did not attend to the significance in it of Jesus Christ as a fundamental, indispensable metaphor. But the question is whether we can understand ourselves and our companions in Christianity or in Christendom, whether we can and do give form to our active existence, with this as our only symbol? In most periods of history there have been Christians who have made the attempt to make Jesus Christ not only the exclusive principle of their understanding but also of their action. But they have never succeeded in doing so, for they have always actually employed other symbolic forms besides. Sometimes they derived these from a Scripture that contains many other words and conveys many other symbolic forms besides this one. Otherwise they derived them from the culture they shared with non-Christians." *The Responsible Self*, pp. 157, 158.

Chapter III. *Shalom:* The Content of the Peaceable City

1. Wolfhart Pannenberg, "Can Christianity Do Without an Eschatology?" *The Christian Hope, Theological Collections, No. 13* (London: S.P.C.K., 1970), pp. 33, 34.
2. Rollo May, *Love and Will* (New York: W. W. Norton & Co., 1969), p. 223.
3. Norman Perrin, *The Kingdom of God in the Teaching of Jesus* (Philadelphia: The Westminster Press, 1963), p. 161.
4. *Ibid.*, p. 162.
5. For a recent review of this question, see Richard H. Hiers, *Jesus and Ethics* (Philadelphia: The Westminster Press, 1968). For the role of the kingdom of God as an eschatological symbol in shaping American church and national history, see H. Richard Niebuhr, *The Kingdom of God in America* (New York: Harper & Brothers, 1937).
6. Perrin, *The Kingdom of God*, p. 187. For Perrin's discussion of the whole question, as referred to in the previous paragraphs, see pp. 158 ff.
7. Wayne G. Rollins, "The New Testament and Apocalyptic," *New Testament Studies*, July, 1971, p. 472.
8. Cf. Hiers, *Jesus and Ethics*, pp. 148-50.
9. Perrin, *The Kingdom of God*, pp. 198, 199.
10. Julio Terán-Dutari, "Peace," *Sacramentum Mundi: An Encyclopaedia of Theology*, 6 vols., ed. by Karl Rahner (Engl. tr., London: Burns & Oates, 1969), V. 4, 380.
11. For specific biblical references one would do well to consult a source as readily available as *The Interpreter's Dictionary of the Bible* (Nashville: Abingdon Press, 1962), V, III, 704 ff. Much of my discussion of the biblical understanding of peace is indebted to the above source, along with the following: *Theological Dictionary of the New Testament*, ed. by Gerhard Kittel, trans. and ed. by Geoffrey W. Bromily (Grand Rapids: Eerdmans Publishing Co., 1964), V. II, 400 ff; Johannes Pederson, *Israel: Its Life and Culture* (London: Oxford University Press), Vols. I, II, 1926, Vols. III, IV, 1940; and Gerhard von Rad, *Old Testament Theology*, trans. by D. M. G. Stalker (London: Oliver & Boyd) V. I, 1962, V. II, 1965.
12. Pederson, *Israel*, V. I-II, 265.
13. Von Rad, *Old Testament Theology*, V. I, 130.
14. Kittel, *Theological Dictionary*, p. 403.
15. *Ibid.*, p. 404.
16. Pederson, *Israel*, p. 287.
17. Cf. von Rad, *Old Testament Theology*, V. II, 169.
18. Gordon D. Kaufman, *Systematic Theology: A Historicist Perspective* (New York: Charles Scribner's Sons, 1968), p. 260.
19. "The Pastoral Constitution on the Church in the Modern World," as cited by Terán-Dutari, "Peace," p. 379.

Chapter IV.   Social Policy and the Experience of *Shalom*

1. Kenneth Underwood, *et al.*, *The Church, the University, and Social Policy* (Middletown, Conn.: Wesleyan University Press, 1969), V. I, 92.
2. Jürgen Moltmann, *Theology of Hope*, trans. by James W. Leitch (London: SCM Press, 1967), p. 21.
3. *Ibid.*, p. 18.
4. *Ibid.*
5. H. Richard Niebuhr, *Christ and Culture* (New York: Harper & Brothers, 1951). Cf. particularly Chapter I, "The Enduring Problem," and esp. pp. 39-44.
6. Rosemary Radford Reuther, *The Radical Kingdom* (New York: Harper & Row, 1970), p. 4. For our discussion, see Chapter I, "The Theology of Revolution and Social Change: The Basic Motifs."
7. *Ibid.*, p. 9.
8. *Ibid.*
9. *Ibid.*, pp. 9, 10.
10. *Ibid.*, p. 14. Cf. Rosemary R. Reuther, "A Radical-Liberal in the Streets of Washington," *Christianity and Crisis*, July 12, 1971, pp. 144-47.
11. Charles C. West, *The Power to Be Human* (New York: The Macmillan Co., 1971), p. 21.
12. *Ibid.*, p. 32.
13. *Ibid.*, p. 142.
14. Peter Worsley, *The Third World*, second edition (Chicago: University of Chicago Press, 1967), p. 77.
15. Underwood, *The Church, the University, and Social Policy*, p. 215. An example of the type of material pertinent to the formulation of the reformist operational model would be the article by Amitai Etzioni, "A Swing to the Right?" *Transaction*, Vol. 7, No. 11 (September, 1970).
16. Albert Camus, *The Plague*, trans. by Stuart Gilbert (New York: Modern Library, 1948), p. 230.

Chapter V.   Hope and Power: Conditions for *Shalom*

1. James M. Gustafson, *Christ and the Moral Life* (New York: Harper & Row, 1968), p. 250.
2. Joseph Haroutunian, "The Christian Hope and the Modern World," *Theology Today*, X, 3 (October, 1953), p. 322.
3. Gustafson, *Christ and the Moral Life*, defines despair as a sin against hope. In our context it is better represented as a lack of trust in God as powerful in his goodness.

4. Johann, *Building the Human*, pp. 152, 153.
5. Haroutunian, "The Christian Hope and the Modern World," p. 324.
6. Johannes B. Metz, *Theology of the World*, trans. by William Glen-Doeppel (New York: Herder and Herder, 1968), p. 92.
7. Moltmann, *Theology of Hope*, pp. 33, 34.
8. *Ibid.*, p. 23.
9. Studs Terkel, *Division Street, America* (New York: Pantheon Books, 1967), p. 10.
10. Chris Argyris, "We Must Make Work Worthwhile," *Life*, May 5, 1967, p. 56.
11. Kenneth Clark, *The Dark Ghetto* (New York: Harper & Row, 1965), pp. 1, 9.
12. Richard N. Goodwin, "Sources of the Public Unhappiness," *The New Yorker*, January 4, 1969, p. 39. This article is a sensitive diagnosis of the malaise of the American political scene of the time.
13. Rollo May, *Love and Will*, p. 31.
14. Paul Tillich, *Love, Power and Justice* (London: Oxford University Press, 1960), p. 87.
15. Hannah Arendt, *The Human Condition* (Garden City, N. Y.: Doubleday Anchor Books, 1959), pp. 219 ff.
16. H. R. Niebuhr, *The Kingdom of God in America*, p. 78.
17. Johann, *Building the Human*, p. 62.

Chapter VI. The Church and *Shalom*

1. The first term, reconciliation, was adopted by the United Presbyterian Church, U.S.A., as a way of signifying the confession of the church in the contemporary period. The second, "the increase of the love of God and neighbor among men," was H. Richard Niebuhr's summary of the purpose of the church in his *The Purpose of the Church and Its Ministry* (New York: Harper & Row, 1956). I have, of course, suggested *shalom* as an apt symbol. Other proposals are "liberation," "revolution," etc.
2. James M. Gustafson, *The Church as Moral Decision-Maker* (Philadelphia: Pilgrim Press, 1970), p. 161.
3. Bonhoeffer, *Ethics*, pp. 30, 41, 42.
4. Henry David Aiken, "The New Morals," *Harper's*, February, 1968, pp. 58, 59.
5. The forward-looking stance energized by an eschatological symbol accords well with the contemporary society on two counts previously unmentioned. One is the presence of permanent change that envelops men today. A concern for the future reflects a consciousness that life will not be as it has been and is. The future is not a problem for societies if

there is no dynamism built into the present and assumed as inevitable. Related to this consciousness of change is the change in scale of interactions present in high-technology cultures. The contemporary society is one of extended interrelationships. Monica Wilson has described the change in outlook that accompanies the shift from isolated and small-scale communities to those that are large-scale and interrelated. "In the small isolated societies the golden age is always in the past, and conservatism which, after all, is a condition of survival in a preliterate society, is highly valued. . . . A large-scale society is quite different. In it the Kingdom of Heaven, or a secular Utopia, lies in the future." Monica Wilson, *Religion and the Transformation of Society* (Cambridge: Cambridge University Press, 1971), pp. 8, 9.

6. For a useful analysis of the church as an organization that requires organizational skills for its own health and for its life with other organizations, see the book referred to earlier by Robert C. Worley, *Change in the Church: A Source of Hope*.

7. St. Augustine in *The City of God* saw the family as the locus for the initial realization of peace. From it, he believed, would radiate the peace required for the social order. That possibility, I am contending, remains, although its realization must not rest on a romantic assumption about the family, nor on a view of the family as the sole source for effecting peace. The family as a source of peace requires diligent and often unspectacular, long-haul work. Such attention is not initially attractive to those who define "where the action is" as in only irruptive locations. But the continuing activity of nurturing selves remains. What counts is the quality of life being sought and provided, whether in dramatic or rather pedestrian "action." For a recent study of the importance of the family for the "moral" attitudes and behavior of children, cf. Douglas Graham, *Moral Learning and Development* (London: B. T. Batsford, 1972), esp. pp. 164 ff.

8. H. R. Niebuhr, *The Responsible Self*, pp. 61, 62.

9. *Ibid.*, p. 167.

10. There are many informative studies about the churches' response to war. Perhaps the most useful remains Roland Bainton, *Christian Attitudes Toward War and Peace* (Nashville: Abingdon Press, 1960). Others are Edward Leroy Long, Jr., *War and Conscience in America* (Philadelphia: The Westminster Press, 1968); and Ralph B. Potter, *War and Moral Discourse* (Richmond: John Knox Press, 1969).

11. Worsley, *The Third World*, pp. 14, 15.

12. Paul VI, *On Fostering the Development of Peoples, Populorum Progressio* (London: Catholic Truth Society, 1968), p. 40.

13. Gustafson, *The Church as Moral Decision-Maker*, p. 61.

Index